Our Daily Bread A History of Barron's Bakery

OUR DAILY

A History of Barron's Bakery

BREAD

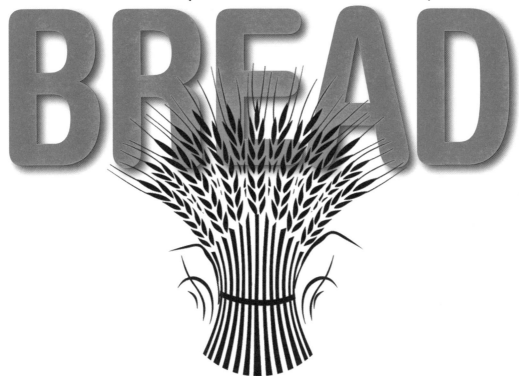

Roz Crowley with photographs by Arna Run Runarsdottir

Published by Onstream 2011

First published in Ireland
by Onstream, Currabaha,
Cloghroe, Co. Cork, Ireland

www.onstream.ie

Author
Roz Crowley

Photography
Arna Run
Runarsdottir

Book design and production
Tony O'Hanlon
Propeller, Galway

Editing and proofreading
Aisling Lyons, Anthony Lee
Cormac O'Dwyer

Printed and bound in Italy
by Graphicom

All efforts have been made
to contact authors of quotations.
Thank you to www.foodreference.com
and www.goodquotes.com and
to individuals for their permission.

ISBN: 978-1-897685-62-4

www.barronsbakery.ie

Foreword
Esther Barron

It has been a great privilege for me to have the opportunity to do a book about the bakery I inherited from my father, Joe Barron. Barron's is a very special bakery for me: as the fourth generation involved, it is not only the family home and a business, but also a way of life. 'Níl aon tinteán mar do thinteán féin', goes the Irish proverb: there is no fireside like your own fireside. There is Barron's Bakery and the Barron family, and it is quite difficult to separate one from the other!

My father had a genuine sense of community. In the Ireland of today this kind of community spirit is very much needed. Thankfully Barron's Bakery has survived for four generations over three centuries. This is due to a consistently good product, a lot of hard work by many people, and taking the good years with the bad. Thanks to our customers' loyal support Barron's Bakery is still thriving. Unfortunately, we have lost most of our small traditional bakeries in Ireland, unlike in France and Italy where they have held on to their tradition of small, local bakeries. Small is beautiful. We need to support our businesses in small towns. In the long term this benefits everybody locally.

This book gives me the opportunity to recognise my mother, my father and Aunt Hess, who brought the bakery through hard times, and from whom I inherited my passion for this wonderful business. They inspired me to keep on the tradition.

9

I wish to thank all those who worked in the bakery over the years and our customers, without them the bakery would not be here today.

This book is extremely important to me and finding Roz Crowley was the perfect fit for many reasons. A big thank you to her for her expertise and experience.

I dedicate this book to my parents, the Barron family, and the people of Cappoquin and the surrounding area.

Introduction
Roz Crowley

I came across Barron's Bakery through an American-Irish friend who was searching in the depths of winter for suitable land to set up a vineyard. He was convinced that grapes for wine-making could be grown in Ireland and was studying microclimates in the hope of finding even a few suitable acres. He stumbled across the bakery in Cappoquin and fell in love with it and the family behind it. When he told me the story I had to see the place for myself.

It was a bakery like no other, with rare brick ovens, old methods of flavour and texture development, and a workplace full of energy. The proprietor, Esther Barron, is a blend of quiet passion, practicality, organisational skills, people management and a good dollop of creativity. She is always thinking, anticipating demand, creating greater demand and innovating to keep ahead of increasing competition from cheaper production methods. The development of the coffee shop with its wonderfully fresh goodies and excellent coffee is a perfect example of her vision. Joined since 1993 by her husband Joe, she is lucky to have beside her someone who has a similar passion for the business, and is full of marketing ideas and the energy of the newly converted. Joe grew up on a farm, is well grounded and aware of how food should taste. Theirs was a good match romantically and, for the future of Barron's Bakery, a perfect one.

Putting together these memories of Barron's bakery has been a huge pleasure. Talking to those who worked there, to customers and those who still value the importance of such an enterprise in their town, I was tempted to incorporate everyone's memories in full into the book. Of course that is not possible but the result, I hope, is a unique celebration of a unique bakery. I have resisted writing another history of Cappoquin, but contributions from those better qualified than I will give you a flavour of the context in which Barron's Bakery developed. I am hugely indebted to Brendan Kiely, Tony McCarthy and Dr Kevin McCarthy for their generosity in supplying me with historical

13

information and lists of sources which helped in piecing together this rich tapestry of a fascinating family. Esther and all the Barron family have been extraordinarily generous with their time, embracing the spirit of sharing information with a great sense of fun that made every interview and exploration sheer pleasure. Later, having interviewed employees and customers from throughout the years, the picture became easy to paint.

Thanks to book designer Tony O'Hanlon, who brought to the book his interpretation of the content to enhance each element with typical flair. As always Aisling Lyons' guiding editorial hand has been a gentle strength.

Placed throughout the book are photographs old and new, showing the development of the bakery to the vibrant entity it is today, worked in by bakers who know exactly what they are doing as they work through the night, wordlessly, to the sound of the radio. I am grateful to a young emerging talent, photographer Arna Run Runarsdottir, for capturing exactly the essence of a night at the bakery in its frantic and graceful beauty; its warmth on camera was more than I could have hoped for. She also managed to do full credit to Mrs Barron's recipes, included at the end of the book, which provided deliciously calorific interludes. These recipes, taken from Mrs Barron's own collection, are favourites of family and friends, and are easy to make and satisfying to serve and enjoy. I have also included some recipes which make the best of leftover bread. Like the Barrons, we should waste nothing, and why would we with the most delicious crumbs at our fingertips?

In Europe almost half of bread production is by craft bakers, yet in Ireland the figure is just one-fifth. All the more reason to celebrate those who, against the odds, continue to stay in business, and have a loyalty to their customers and a deep commitment to quality and service.

Four Generations: A Family Bakery

John and Hanora Barron, 1925

Cappoquin is a small river town at the head of the Blackwater Navigation in Co. Waterford. It was here, in 1887, that John Barron established one of Ireland's oldest, and most celebrated bakeries, Barron's.

Bounded by three bridges, the Stone, the Red and the Little, Cappoquin nestles into one of the foothills of the Knockmealdown Mountains on the main road from Killarney to Rosslare. It has always been a strategic town for commerce: the Blackwater River provided transport, bringing coal from Wales, taking away timber used for pit-props, and serving the iron-ore industries. It was formerly on the main Cork to Dublin route. Between 1878 and 1967 a railway line handled passengers and freight between Mallow and Rosslare, supporting a strong industrial base and bringing prosperity to many families.

The Barron family has a long history in Co. Waterford. The first Barron recorded in Cappoquin was John, born in 1792, died in 1847 who was married to Ellen (Elleanor) Fitzgerald. In 1810 John Barron is recorded as a publican on Main Street. They had eight children: James, Ellen, Mary, Brigid, Margaret, Janet and Michael. Their third child John, started a bakery on Main Street, quite likely in the same premises as the pub, which was commonplace in those days.

However, it is back with their first son, James, that we find what was to become the longest line of bakers in the family. James married Mary Connors and had eight children. They had a shop with general provisions and an oven in which bread was baked for sale in the shop only. There were anything up to twenty premises of this kind in Cappoquin and also more fully-fledged bakeries with brick ovens made from local bricks in Coolfin and Youghal. The bread would go straight on top of the bricks which were heated with coals pushed around the sides of the oven. The oven would be cleaned out with a scuffle, a large sack tied to a pole and dipped in water. Up to that time, it was commonplace for the rural kitchens of poorer people not to have ovens, so Irish soda bread would be cooked over the fire in a bastible, a cast-iron pot which served as a small oven. In her excellent *A Little History of Irish Food* (Gill & Macmillan, Dublin, 1998) food historian Regina Sexton tells of the great respect and appreciation that a table laden with bread would receive in the upper echelons of society.

17

New York, December 13th 1886

My Dearest Nora,

I hope you and the little darling are well and after spending a happy Christmas for I know this letter will not reach you until after that feast day.

Dearest Nora I cannot tell you how put out I am for not having a letter from you before this but I suppose it is the weather is the cause of it. I feel very lonesome at this festival for a good many reasons but it will be the last with God's help. I slept very uneasy those few nights back. I hope you gave the dues for the dead which I am sure you did.

Dearest Nora I suppose in a few days I will have your letter and will be able to decide when I will go home after getting out this place would not do me at all. Though the wages is fair it is too cold for me and it is only a temperate place. I only asked it for a short time but anyhow I am better off than to go home the time I was to go.

Dear Nora this is my New Years card to you and baby 3 pounds. I got some winter clothing. I wanted them we had a very heavy fall of snow here the cold is terrible. I will expect you to see your and mine, and entrust I will be ready for home. I expect a lot of good news in the letter that is due from you and I will see my way for home then. I hope Patey is well and all. My sister Maggie would like to have you and baby Rose. She had a letter from Wexford from the little sisters and they told her you write to them often. I was so glad.

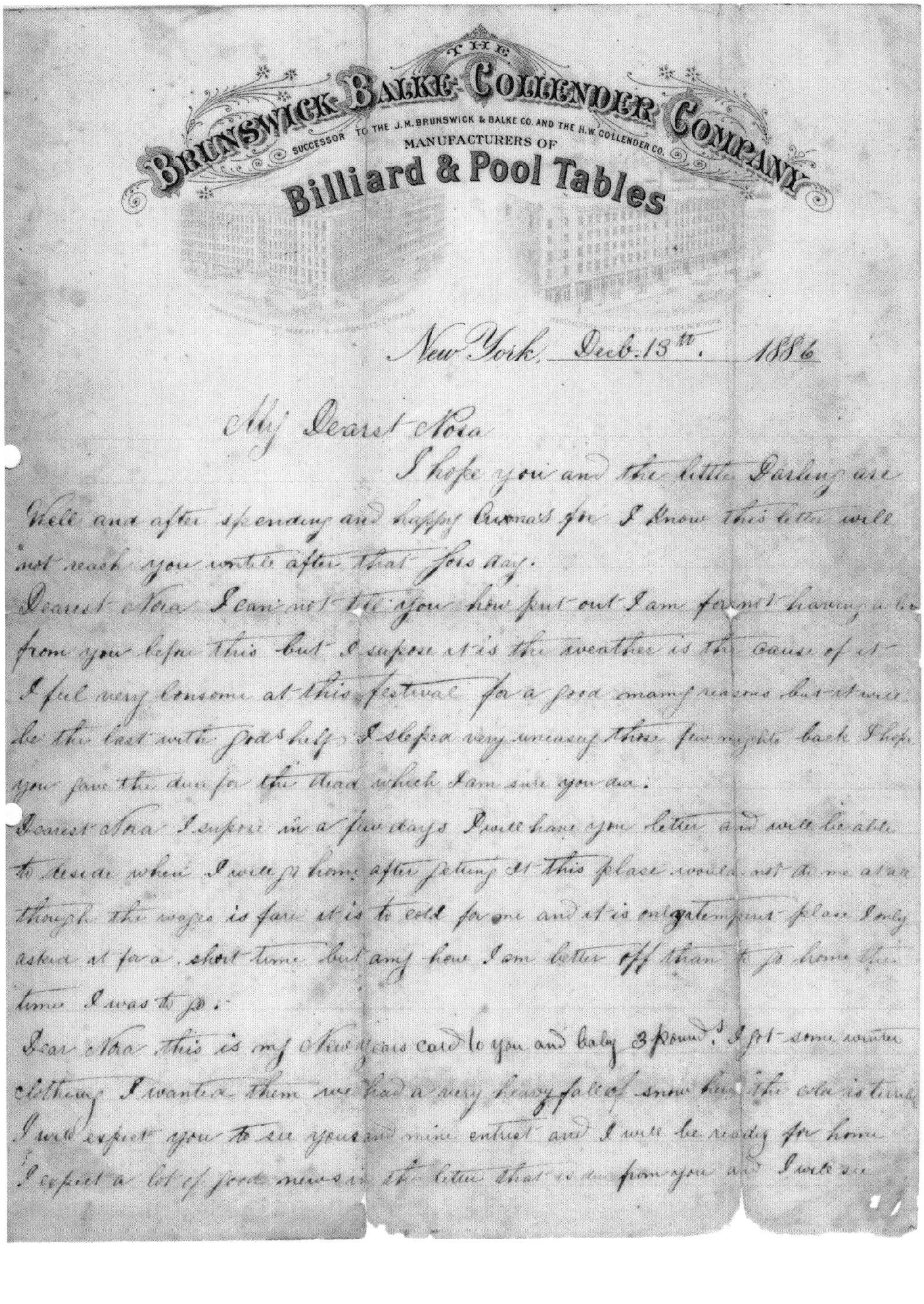

THE
BRUNSWICK-BALKE-COLLENDER COMPANY
SUCCESSOR TO THE J.M. BRUNSWICK & BALKE CO. AND THE H.W. COLLENDER CO.
MANUFACTURERS OF
Billiard & Pool Tables

New York, Decb. 13th 1886

My Dearst Nora

I hope you and the little Darling are
well and after spending and happy Cxmmas for I know this letter will
not reach you untile after that fois day.

Dearest Nora I can not tell you how put out I am for not having a le__
from you before this but I supose it is the weather is the cause of it
I feel very lonsome at this festival for a good many reasons but it will
be the last with gods help I sleped very uneasy these few nights back I hope
you gave the due for the dead which I am sure you did.

Dearest Nora I supose in a few days I will have you letter and will be able
to deside when I will go home after geting it this place would not do me at all
though the wages is fare it is to cold for one and it is onlytemporis place I only
asked it for a short time but any how I am better off than to go home the
time I was to go.

Dear Nora this is my New years card to you and baby 3 pounds I got some winter
clothing I wanted them we had a very heavy fall of snow her the cold is terrible
I will expect you to see yours and mine entrest and I will be ready for home
I expect a lot of good news in the letter that is due from you and I will se

Dearest Nora I thought I would have another hunt on Keane's estate by this time it will not be long. I suppose Geary is well, have he had the op yet? How is Murray. I am sure he often speaks of me the poor old fellow, tell him I have seen Gillmore's band several times, tell him it would be a new life to him to hear it they are nearly all Irish in it. There is no mistake but it is a fine band the best in the world.

Dear Nora how is Ellen Collender getting on have she the house yet. Tell me in your next letter give me a lot of news in your letter. I suppose the little darling is getting very big now. I like to see her and live happy forever until death end. How is the baking with you at present. Tell me about Burks, was there any change there since. Try and learn how they will get on with the cakes from me. Let me know all and a long letter, and after you may expect me home. I see Inla very often she is well she wants to know when I am going home for some thing she have to bring I think. If you like I will get you a ring send me the size though I can give a good guess to it for it is the same ring fit us so tell me in your next letter. I just send you this paper till you see a sketch of the factory you will tell me about the house how is it you paid no rent give me all accounts in the letter I suppose I will have a lot in the next one. Joe Cleary gave me some things to bring home I have them safe. Tell Katy I suppose I will be the giver still of them. Tell Mrs Gillian it was a great pity there was a strike in James's shop he is idle at present do not forget it. Also tell me where Bridget McGrath is, he like to know as not speak of it to any one. Remember he asked me to ask you for he have a reason find it out. Dear Nora send some little present to the little ones for me in my name. It would be too expensive of me from here now. Dearest Nora I think I have told you all for the present. Hoping to see you soon with God's help. Remember me to all and Reverend Mother with fond love to you and my little darling.

I remain Dearest Nora

Your fond Husband Johney

20

My way for home then I hope Baby is well and all My sister Maggie
would like to have you and baby [...] she had a letter from Wexford from
the little sisters and she tola her you wrote to them often I was so [...]
Dearest Nha I thought I would have a nother hunt on Keanes estate
by this time it will not be long I supose Peary is well have he the [...]
yet how is Murray I am sure he often speaks of [...] the [...] felow tele
him I have seen Gilmores band several times tele him it would be a
new life to him to here it they are nearly all Irish in it there is no mistake
but it is a fine band the best in the world.
Dear Nha how is Ellen Collender geting on have she the house yet tele
me in your next letter give me a lot of news in your letter I supose the little darling
is geting very big now I like to see her and live happy for ever untill death [...]
how is the baking with you at presant tele me about Burks was there any
change there since they and learn how they geting on with the cakes for me
let me know all and a long letter and after you may expect me home [...]
see [...] very often she is well she want to [...] when I am going home for [...]
thing she [...] to bring I think If you like I will get you a ring send me the
size though I can give a good gess to it for it is the same ring fits us
so tele me in your next letter I last sent you this paper tele you see
a sketch of the factory you will tele me about the house how is it you
payed no rent give me all accounts in the letter I supose I will have a lot
in the next [...] Ive Oleary gave me something to bring home I have them safe
tele Katy I supose I will see the poor state of them tele Mrs Gillian it was
a great pity there was a strik in James [...] he is [...] at presant do not
forget it all tele me when Buyer [...] is he like to know do not speak
of it to any one remember he asked me to aske you for he have a reason find it
out dear Nha [...] some little presant to the little ones for me in my name
it would be to expensive of me from here now dearest Nha I think I have
tola you all with the presant hoping to see you soon with gods help remember
me to all and [...] Mother with fond love to you and my little darling
I remain Dearest Nha
your fond Husband John [...]

John Barron and son Joe

On Main Street, between Keane's Iron Foundry and the barracks, was the fever hospital where many died. Even with the great advances in medicine in the Victorian era, deadly diseases like cholera could still strike in small towns such as Cappoquin. Mary and James Barron died within weeks of each other of Typhoid fever as the year turned from 1881 to 1882; James was in Lismore fever hospital, Mary at home in Main Street.

James had paid £50 for his son John's (known as John James) apprenticeship in O'Keeffe's Bakery in Touraneena. Baking was a well-respected and controlled craft and Master Baker was a fine title to have. Kneading, shaping and timing ovens was all precision work. Yeast was recognised as being difficult to work with and in the wrong hands it could cause chaos in the bakery. It took John five years to complete the apprenticeship. As well as a trade, John left O'Keeffe's with a wife, Hanorah (Norah) Collender, who he had met as he walked home across the fields from Touraneena to Cappoquin. The couple married in 1885.

However, John was a reluctant baker and had only gone into the business to please his father. Itchy feet carried him to America, where cousins of his wife, the Collenders, had a number of businesses. Hugh Collender, born in December 1829, had supported the insurrection against British rule and fled to the USA. He married the daughter of Michael Phelan who was a partner in the Brunswick Balke Collender Billiard Company. Hugh became a multi-millionaire and was so well thought of that he got a dispensation to have his funeral in St Patrick's Cathedral, New York, on Good Friday 1890. He was well thought of at home too, providing employment to many emigrants from Cappoquin. Michael Barron, Joe Barron's older brother, used to say that so many had gone to the United States he hardly had any relatives in Ireland.

John James had seven siblings and followed most of them to New York in search of a life that was far more comfortable than that at home. Norah intended to join him when he was settled but when the couple's first child, Mary Rose, was born, she decided she couldn't leave home after all. John returned from New York to his wife Norah and his newborn daughter in Cappoquin within the year. He opened the bakery in 1887 in its existing location on the Square, further developing the site behind the house. The couple went on to have four daughters and eight sons – twelve children in all – just short of the baker's dozen!

In 1930, John died and his wife Norah retired to their house in Ballinameela and died in 1952. The bakery was passed on to the eldest son still at home, Jack Barron. Born in 1890, Jack saw himself as an entrepreneur and more 'management' than 'hands-on'. He bought Harrington's Hotel on Cook Street in 1930. In 1938, Jack's wife May (Daly) died, the hotel went downhill and was sold out of the family. His brother Joe, who had the required experience and work ethic, as well as a love of the industry, was the ideal candidate to take over the bakery.

Born in 1904, Joe Barron had worked in the bakery from the age of fourteen. He did not have the opportunity of a secondary education and in a perfect world, with a love of the English language, would have been a journalist. Times were tough and there was competition. In 1929, the year of the Wall Street Crash, *Thoms Directory* lists six bakeries in Cappoquin: Barron's of the Square, Bateman's of Main St., Dunne's of Main St., Kenny's of Main St., McCarthy's of Barrack St. and Stanley's of Main St. It also has two confectioners: Treacy and Dunne of Main St. and Gerard Watson of Main St.

23

Brothers Hugh and Joe Barron

The Saddlers Coffee Shop

Joe and Joan Barron at their wedding in 1943

In 1943 Joe married Joan, the daughter of Andrew Hickey, a businessman in Lismore who had a hardware shop, car hire business and a garage. He was also a member of Lismore Town Commissioners for many years. Joan would have absorbed a feel for business but her privileged background would not have prepared her for the hard graft ahead. She took it with good grace, however, driving the delivery van when necessary and keeping an eye on the business in general, often a comforting ear and provider of warm soup for staff members working late. All of this while producing five daughters who, as they got older and were needed, worked in the business at one time or another.

This was a time of mixed fortunes in Cappoquin. The Second World War brought misfortune to many families who were left without fathers, husbands and sons. Poverty was commonplace, large families were reared in tiny cottages, farms provided a basic living and families helped each other to survive. The late 1940s and 1950s was an interesting era in Cappoquin with many small businesses, some supporting those with a relatively comfortable lifestyle. There were the tailors, Ned and his sons Thomas and Noel Lonergan, who sat cross-legged in the window of their premises, and Pete Cahill just across the road from them; Geoff Gambon, a shoemaker; Keating's saddlery; John Rea, a blacksmith; Connolly barbers; and the bacon and chicken factories.

Joe with brothers Michael and
Gerald Barron

Barron family. Gerald Barron
(Joe's brother), Hess (Joe's sister)
Back:Joe, Joan. Front: daughters
Margo, Noreen, Deirdre and
Siobhan

The train line still serviced the area, bringing
an influx of visitors to the monastery at
Mount Melleray and arriving with provisions for businesses, including the bakery.
By 1951 Barron's was the only bakery left
in Cappoquin, although Treacey and
Dunne on Main Street were, like Barron's,
listed as confectioners, while Bateman's,
Lincoln's and McCarthy's, once listed as
bakers, were called corn merchants.

Cappoquin was still a typical market town,
and the bakery was central to its economy.

Joe and Joan were joined in the business
by Joe's sister, Hesther, who ran the shop
in front of the bakery. Like the rest of the
family, Hesther lived over the premises
and kept everyone in check, balancing
Joe's empathy and generosity with a more
businesslike eye on the running of the
business, especially its finances. She was
known to be quite a character.
The bakery prospered with the help of
families and individuals such as the
Meskills, Willie McGrath and John Crowley,
and in latter years the Murrays, Paddy,
Milo and Denis. The business grew along
with the increase in demand for 'shop
bread', and new distribution routes were
set up to reach customers in outlying areas.

25

Joe Barron outside the bakery, 1940

Joe was the first Irishman to become a member of the Guild of British Bakers. An artisan baker, he was not interested in money, but in producing good quality bread and providing for his wife and five daughters, making sure they received the education not afforded to him. He educated himself, constantly reading books on a wide range of topics, doing his best to pass on his knowledge with questions and answers not always appreciated by his lively daughters. His father had first delivered bread in his pony and trap, and Joe bought a van and continued the service, later employing van drivers. His daughters also replaced him when he became arthritic. But there was fun for him too, and with a rich sonorous voice, he sang in the local choir, played in the local brass band and was a sports enthusiast. When he could get away from work he occasionally enjoyed a swim and to row on the local Blackwater river. He was deeply religious, heading annual events such as the Corpus Christi procession. The rosary was said every day in the household and a strict code of morals and sense of community manifested itself in a genuine awareness that his bounty should be shared with those less fortunate.

Joe Barron died in 1980 at the age of seventy-six. He left the bakery to his daughter Esther, who had joined him five years previously. Esther married Joe Prendergast in 1993, and together they have carried on the business into its third century.

Deirdre Hallahan (Barron) and Joan Barron

The town was enjoying mixed fortunes when Esther took over in 1980. Cappoquin Bacon Factory, which had been a large employer since 1907, was absorbed into Lunham's factory in Cork. A second bacon factory survived for a further ten years, along with Cappoquin Chickens, another employer full of good bakery customers. Small shops and craftspeople closed up. In some cases, when a craftsperson such as a tailor died, there was no-one to replace him; others were not able to survive a fast-changing marketplace.

But nothing daunted the Barrons. They had space for a commercial enterprise in which a good variety of bread could be produced throughout the night to satisfy the needs of their community. Customers responded well to innovation and appreciated the deep taste and aromas of a decent loaf of bread, handmade by bakers who knew their craft.

In the 1940s Joe Barron had updated the bakery, buying labour-saving machinery such as mixers and provers, and converting the ovens from wood to oil in the two existing Scotch brick ovens. Delivered from Glasgow, their large double metal doors fronted walls built of red, fired brick. The ovens were dome-shaped for good air circulation and had an inside cavity of about twelve feet square. They worked on the same principle as the first ovens used by the Egyptians 3,000 years ago. These same, labour-intensive ovens are in use today; expensive to run and requiring great skill to operate, but producing bread of unique flavour and crust.

Barron's bread is baked on a 'falling heat' for an hour. First, the ovens are internally fired to reach a temperature of about 600 degrees Fahrenheit. This takes between an hour and a half and two hours. The oven is then switched off and sealed, so its thick brick walls absorb and retain the heat. Next the oven is loaded: proved, hand-moulded loaves in black metal loaf tins, moulded together in 'straps' of four, are pushed into the oven using nine-foot long wooden-handled peels. By the time the oven is fully loaded, the temperature has fallen to about 475 degrees Fahrenheit. The bread bakes as the temperature continues to drop.

The oven is operated without a thermostat. It takes an enormous amount of skill and dedication to understand and manage not only the temperature of the oven, but also the many other factors that affect the final product, such as the flour and the ambient temperature of the bakery. Of course, the capricious Irish weather means the humidity and outside temperatures are unpredictable; this means that both the ingredients and the ovens behave differently from day to day. From season to season, and with every new harvest, the moisture content of the flour changes, and so must the recipe. Traditionally, flour was judged simply by touch and smell, but today the bakers communicate as much as possible with the millers to gain the best understanding of their main ingredient.

These days the flour is a blend of wheat from Canada, the UK and Germany, milled in Belfast by Andrews Milling, Waterford Flour Mills (Heart's Delight), Odlums in Dublin and Kells in Kilkenny. In the earlier days there were far more flour mills and Joe Barron dealt with many of them – Davis of Enniscorthy, Mosses of Bennetsbridge, Barrow Milling in Carlow, National, Waterford, and Shackleton Flour Mills in Lucan.

Even within a single batch, not all loaves are the same – near the walls the temperature is higher, so the bread will be especially crusty; some customers prefer softer loaves from the centre of the oven or nearer the door. The final variable is the hand of the baker who makes the bread. Esther says that even with the same ingredients, the same oven, the same conditions, she will know who made the scones on a given day. The baker's character goes into the bread.

It is the slow bake in these ovens that gives Barron's bread a unique taste and crust. The bread undergoes a long, slow proving and extensive hand-moulding, which also contributes to the flavour. This bread takes time, and it is a far cry from the mass-produced bread product eaten so often today.

Modern, factory-produced bread may be baked for less than twenty minutes. Par-baked bread is partially baked, deep-frozen and later baked off. Rather than the slow fermentation of craft-baked bread, the proving process is hastened in the modern bakery by intense mechanical agitation in high-speed mixers, so there is no time for the full flavours to be expressed. This process also allows the flour to absorb more water. Small wonder that such bread is additive-laden – the taste has to come from somewhere. Preservatives also mean the bread may take weeks to go off. Why has such bread come to dominate the market? Research has shown that consumers buy bread that they can squeeze – if the bread on the shelf is not yielding enough, they will leave it behind. Ironically, well-baked bread does not squeeze well! Furthermore, price-conscious consumers are unwilling to pay the price for good bread. It's a vicious circle: fewer customers means fewer bakeries, which in turn means less awareness of – and demand for – good bread.

Barron's survival has ensured that its customers have been continuously offered an alternative to what celebrity cook Nigella Lawson calls 'plastic bread', but not without facing the same challenges as craft bakeries throughout the country. Pressure on small bakeries began in the 1950s and 1960s with competition from large, national bakeries. Many were affected such as confectioners Thompson's of Cork, Power's, Dee's, Tom Hayes and Moloney's of Dungarvan, Hill's of Kilmacthomas and

The Barron sisters:
Noreen (Cormican), Margo (Murphy),
Siobhan (McCarthy), Deirdre (Hallahan),
and Esther Barron.

Madder's of Portlaw. Such pressure intensified with the growth of large and powerful supermarkets, whose aggressive trading practices and enormous purchasing power have constituted the greatest threat to the craft bakery. The related demise of the small shop has made bakeries even more dependent on supermarkets as their way of reaching the customer. Price wars and aggressive supermarkets in the 1980s were at first harmful to small bakeries, but later saw that some relatively smaller bakeries could supply them with the quality bread demanded by consumers. In the 1990s, food production legislation added to the burden on bakeries. The implementation of HACCP hygiene-related legislation, for example, was just too expensive for many small producers, and meant that it was no longer viable for them to continue trading.

During the 1990s, Esther was almost ready to give up due to the mammoth task of finding good staff. Sadly, young Irish people were no longer interested in working in a bakery. Long, unsociable hours looked decidedly unattractive compared with easier work and conditions elsewhere. In France, Switzerland and many central and eastern European countries there is great appreciation of the skills of the baker and the status of the baker is that of the professional. Unfortunately, in Ireland we have some way to go to accord our Irish bakers the same respect. The cost of wages at a time when margins are tight further compounds the challenge. But talented Filipino bakers have been found and nowadays they work alongside Eastern Europeans and Irish bakers to make up a staff with a decidedly global quality.

Esther Barron studied Domestic Science and worked for six months in a restaurant before joining her father Joe at the bakery in the 1970s. She was keen to develop the business and quickly added a confectionary department. Within a year of inheriting the business in 1980, she bought adjoining premises, and in 1983 opened a coffee shop. Three years later, the staff at Barron's had increased from three to ten. The bakery now delivers within an eleven-mile radius to Dungarvan farmers' market, and shops and supermarkets in Tallow, Ballyduff, Lismore, Cappoquin, Dungarvan, Aglish, Villierstown, Conna, Youghal, Ardkeen and Yellow Road, Waterford city.

Food critic John McKenna of The Bridgestone Guides was among the first to communicate Esther and Joe's passion to a wider audience, and many food writers have celebrated the bakery since. The earlier growth in demand for 'shop bread', since eroded by the increasing dominance of factory bread, has been mirrored in the more recent upsurge of interest in artisan bakeries. Consumers are more conscious of quality and health. We increasingly realise that when all bread was baked traditionally, and when wheat was grown with fewer chemicals, there was very little evidence of people being allergic to wheat or yeast. Craft bread is now sought out by those with special dietary requirements and Barron's makes bread with rye and spelt flour to cater to these customers.

29

The growth in popularity of farmers' markets has been another boon for Barron's, as it has for other craft bakeries and small producers. Farmers' markets allow producers to sell their products directly to consumers. The Dungarvan Farmers' Market was set up in June 2004; Barron's Bakery sells there every Thursday morning. For them, it is a way to get to know customers and their preferences, and to direct new customers to the shops in Dungarvan that stock their products the other five days of the week.

Other changes in the daily life of the bakery have allowed it to meet the larger-scale changes within the baking industry. The working day, for example, no longer starts early each morning; today work begins at 8pm and continues through the night, so that the products are ready to fill supermarket shelves at 7.30am. The product range has also changed and expanded. Nowadays many customers expect their loaves to be sliced and wrapped, which adds another step to the process. The bakery is helping to bring back to life traditional treats such as Chester cake and gingerbread. Another constant is the Waterford blaa, a traditional Waterford bread bun. The blaa gets its name from blanc, the French word for white, or it may be from blé, the French word for wheat. It has been produced in Waterford city and county since the time of the Huguenots in the 1600s. Traditionally made without preservatives, it is best eaten for breakfast or lunch, and so remains relatively unknown outside Waterford.

Barron's continues to produce traditional loaves, such as tile bread, cooked directly on the sole of the oven. Turnovers are a hand-moulded sliced pan loaf, and a pan is an unsliced loaf with the traditional rounded top with a crust; it is loved by many when it is almost burned to a toffee crispness. The attractive basket pan is also hand-moulded and hand-shaped with its distinctive s-shape before being baked in its basket-shaped tin. There are also cobs, round hand-shaped loaves, seed loaves, plain loaves, soda bread and spotted dog (white soda with fruit in it), as well as Irish barm brack. An increasingly cosmopolitan staff and clientele have led to the addition of sourdough, multiseed, spelt and rye bread. Customers are loyal to the bakery and have been served well by staff members who remember just how they like their bread. Throughout the years customer service has been key to Barron's success. When some of his customers didn't have large enough ovens, or needed them for their roast potatoes, Joe Barron invited his customers to use his ovens for their turkeys at Christmas. This meant he didn't get a full day off, even on Christmas Day, and was still up at 7am to light the ovens.

Cappoquin brass band 1925. Joe Barron, with hat, back row, second from right.

The bakery has been recognised with a raft of awards, both national and international. These have given the bakery a further boost, leading to appearances in the papers and on radio. In the first Blas na hÉireann National Food Awards in 2008, Barron's Bakery won the Gold Award in the bread section with their Country Style bread, which has a four-hour fermentation period. They shared first place with Blazing Salads Bakery of Dublin. Minister for Horticulture and Food, Trevor Sargent, presented the Barrons with an impressive piece of Dingle crystal. In 2002, the Barrons were honoured by the French Confraternity of Master Bakers (La Confrérie des Talmeliers du Bon Pain) during the Fête du Four baking festival at Cappoquin's twin town of Chanat-la-Mouteyre in the Auvergne region of France. The local guild of bakers, dressed in their ceremonial robes representing the colour and crust of bread, invited Esther and Joe to eat a ceremonial loaf. They were tapped on both shoulders with a specially designed oven peel, before being presented with a medal and scroll. As a result of the twinning, and inspired by Barron's ovens, Chanat revived their community oven during its Fête du Four festival. At this time their big ovens are open to the public to bake their own loaves.

Barron's Bakery won first place in the Craft Bread section at the Bakex (Skillnets) 2005 competition in the RDS. In 2006, Esther and Joe represented Ireland at the Festa del Pane in Savigliano, Piedmont, Italy. And in 2008, Barron's was one of four Waterford bakeries which were recognised for their regional bread at the Taste Festivals/Eurotoques Food Awards for the humble Waterford blaa.

Students from Ballymaloe Cookery School have visited Barron's to see the ovens and soak up the passion that has allowed the Barrons to keep making craft bread after so many have had to give up. Barron's bread even appeared in the 1983 film version of William Trevor's *One of Ourselves*; several hundred loaves appeared as extras in a scene shot in the bakery. Fortunately for the coffee shop, opened just weeks beforehand, the film crew needed lots of coffee and plenty of sweet sustenance. The timing couldn't have been better.

The bakery has also been featured on food programmes such as *Corrigan Knows Food*, Éamonn Ó'Catháin's *Bia's Bóthar*, Clodagh McKenna's *Fresh from the Farmers' Market*, *Nationwide* and TG4's *Ar Bhóitharín na Smaointe*. Author Colman Andrews included Barron's recipe for Chester Cake in *The Country Cooking of Ireland*.

While the Irish consumer's interest in good bread has grown, Esther hopes that growth will continue in the future. Comparisons are often made between Ireland and the continent, where small bakeries are given greater recognition, and where bread is associated with prosperity, rather than being dismissed as a poor man's food. In Italy, craft bakeries have ninety per cent of the market share, while in Ireland it is only fifteen per cent. Through her term as president of the Flour Confectioner's and Baker's Association (FCBA), Esther worked to safeguard her craft and ensure its continued success. During her presidency, the FCBA was affiliated with the International Union of Bakers and Baking Confectioners. The FCBA also became involved in Skillnets, a government-funded training and upskilling scheme. To further underline their commitment to quality, local food traditions, they are members of Good Food Ireland and committee members of the Food Safety Authority of Ireland.

Underpinning Barron's success is a simple passion for good bread, handed down through four generations. But above all, the Barrons have been unfailing in their recognition of the role of the local community in keeping the bakery alive.

Joe Prendergast and Esther Barron,
President FCBA 2003

33

Family Tree
JOHN BARRON

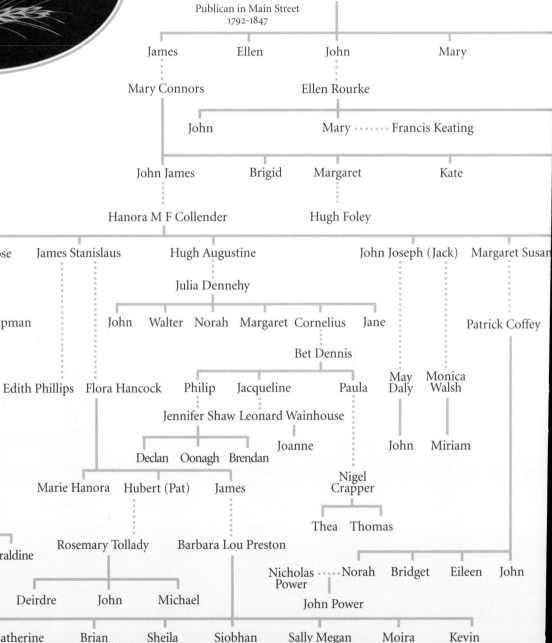

John Barron · · · · · · · · Eleanor (Ellen) Fitzgerald
Publican in Main Street
1792-1847

James   Ellen   John   Mary

Mary Connors   Ellen Rourke

John   Mary · · · · · · Francis Keating

John James   Brigid   Margaret   Kate

Hanora M F Collender   Hugh Foley

Mary Rose   James Stanislaus   Hugh Augustine   John Joseph (Jack)   Margaret Susan

Julia Dennehy

34

Thomas Chapman   John   Walter   Norah   Margaret   Cornelius   Jane   Patrick Coffey

Bet Dennis

Edith Phillips   Flora Hancock   Philip   Jacqueline   Paula   May Daly   Monica Walsh

Jennifer Shaw   Leonard Wainhouse

Joanne   John   Miriam

Declan   Oonagh   Brendan

Marie Hanora   Hubert (Pat)   James   Nigel Crapper

Thea   Thomas

Rosemary Tollady   Barbara Lou Preston

Peter John   Geraldine   Nicholas Power · · · · · Norah   Bridget   Eileen   John

Deirdre   John   Michael   John Power

Patricia Catherine   Brian   Sheila   Siobhan   Sally Megan   Moira   Kevin

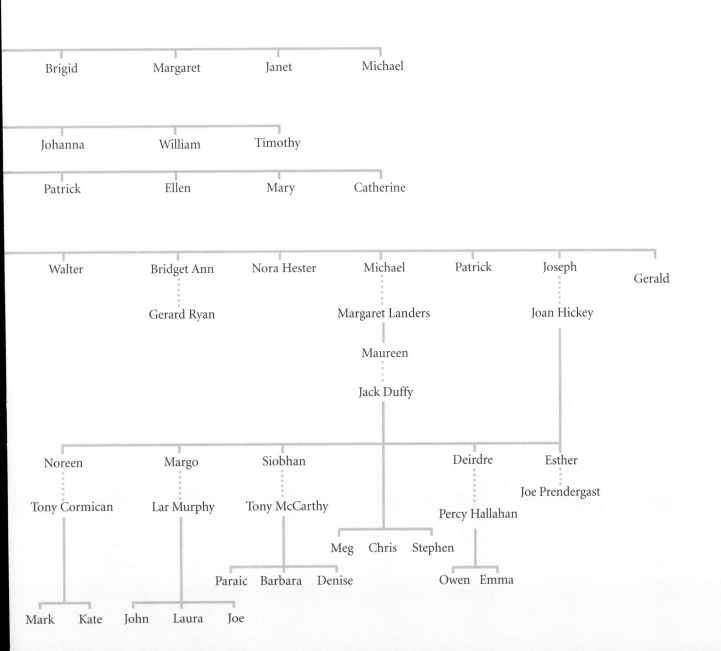

Brigid   Margaret   Janet   Michael

Johanna   William   Timothy

Patrick   Ellen   Mary   Catherine

Walter   Bridget Ann   Nora Hester   Michael   Patrick   Joseph   Gerald

Gerard Ryan   Margaret Landers   Joan Hickey

Maureen

Jack Duffy

Noreen   Margo   Siobhan   Deirdre   Esther

Tony Cormican   Lar Murphy   Tony McCarthy   Joe Prendergast

Percy Hallahan

Meg   Chris   Stephen

Paraic   Barbara   Denise   Owen   Emma

Mark   Kate   John   Laura   Joe

The Aroma of History:
Memories from the Barron Family

Esther Barron

I studied domestic science at Beaufort House, Rathfarnham, Dublin. For six months I worked as manageress in Adam & Eve's restaurant in Cork, which was a good training for coming home to the business. My dream was to build the business, which at the time had just one baker and a van man employed, while my mother ran the bread shop.

My first decision was to employ someone to run the shop and relieve my mother of this task. I had had five years in the bakery with my father and liked the finance and management side of the business. I started baking confectionery every day at 7am starting with soda bread and scones. Dad was still passionate about the bakery but was getting too old for the work. I inherited his passion and wanted to see it continue, and my enthusiasm gave him the spur to invest in a flour silo, which was labour and cost effective. He was happy to invest and had confidence in the future. It was important to him to see it going on. He always wanted a son and I think I became that person for him. I was passionate and focused on a career but I still found time to have a social life at the weekends. Mother would tip me under the table when I was telling him about race meetings where I might get up to mischief. As I used to say, 'All work and no play makes Jack a dull boy!' He was passionate and used to say, 'If the product is good, I'm happy.'

Artisans are moody people and are influenced by how their product turns out every day. Daddy always bought the best ingredients and if flour came and had low protein content, he would be annoyed with the millers for not informing him. Canadian wheat is best for bread and ours comes from Canada and also some from France, Germany and the UK.

Within five years I built up the staff to ten which was a big step forward for a business I loved. My sister Margo had started extending the confectionery lines in the bakery and she trained me in. She was a great support to me at that time.

We gradually increased production to employing three confectioners. At the time doughnuts, éclairs, cheesecakes and black forest gateaux were fashionable. Margo suggested that our father leave the bakery to me. It was logical: I wasn't married and as I had worked in it, was able to take it on. Easter weekend was the busiest of the year, even busier than Christmas, when people bought confectionery treats as gifts. We were never busier than in the 1980s – a great time for the bakery when I had three working exclusively on confectionery. The coffee shop was the next to come on stream in 1983. I had bought the saddlery next door in 1980 and it took time to develop. Aunt Hess died in 1967 and Father died in 1980.

Esther and Joe in front of the ovens

Hess thought Father wasn't tough enough, so she had to make up for it. Aunt Hess was older than Daddy and she took responsibility for the finance end of the business. She loved the family and was good to us. On her day off, she used to take the train to Cork, do some shopping and bring home presents to us. I was called after her, and Noreen and I were her favourites.

Daddy always believed in leaving his money locally. 'Put your money where you get it. Cut your cloth according to your measure and save for what you want,' he'd say. He would buy suits from Jimmy Olden, the local draper. When Jimmy suggested it would be easier for him if Daddy got his own in Cork, Daddy still believed that if Jimmy had a rack of suits, it would attract more business. Even our cars were bought through a local man, Austin Sargent, so that Austin could get his percentage even though it was cheaper to buy from the main dealer. There were five drapery shops in Cappoquin when I was a child and I particularly remember lovely jumpers in O'Shea's shop window. The other drapers were Grace O'Connor, Kingston's and Mary Kerfoot's.

The idea with the coffee shop was to give added value to bread – good sandwiches with soup, nice tea and coffee with the cakes. It was the first coffee shop in town. I was even congratulated on my optimism for tourism in developing a site which had been derelict for years. I was delighted to provide somewhere to have a chat.

The Barron sisters: Noreen Cormican, Margo Murphy, Siobhan McCarthy, Deirdre Hallahan, Esther Barron

Paddy Murray, best known as The Baker, ran the bread bakery like clockwork. He produced a consistently high quality loaf and served his time with my father for almost 25 years. Milo, his brother, was on the van and was thoroughly reliable too. All the Murray family had a great association with the bakery. Another great baker was Dermot Dee from Dungarvan. When I ran the business on my own right through the 1980s, I had an excellent core staff, especially the many young women in the shop and on confectionery.

My father was a great community man in many ways. Cappoquin has a thriving community spirit with a wide range and number of local organisations, including the Cappoquin Community Development company of which I was a founder member. We are all very proud of the wonderful community centre that they have built. The reestablished Tidy Town association has also added greatly to the town.

When the coffee shop was opened first, the square opposite had been neglected for many years. But all the neighbours got together and planted flowers, and we meet one evening a week to maintain it. In 2005 when the bakery won a national bread award, I was so overwhelmed and appreciative of all the local goodwill that, along with Joe, I decided that we must thank the community for their good wishes.

Out of that grew the annual Cappoquin Cornerstone Carnival and this year it celebrated its sixth anniversary which was the best one yet. In recent years Cappoquin Civic Link, the heritage group, and many other events and activities have developed and as a Cappoquin person, I am proud to record their contribution to life in Cappoquin. My husband Joe brought marketing skills to the bakery. We make a very good team. His energy knows no bounds.

39

Joe Prendergast

You can butter, but you cannot better Barron's bread

I had been sales manager with World Book Encyclopedia and met Esther in 1991. We married eighteen months later. I immediately found the business interesting. With the advent of computers, the book business was changing and Esther and I felt that a career together would work. Esther trained me in to manage the bakery. My grandmother had always baked lovely brown bread and my mother continues the tradition.

I always remember my first morning in the bakery, when Esther was introducing me to the products. I was fascinated and confused by all the different pans, their names and shapes. I had previously worked with Macra na Feirme in Co. Waterford, so I already knew many people in the area. I settled in very quickly to Cappoquin and I found everybody very friendly and helpful to me. Esther's mother, Joan, was a most friendly person and very easy to get on with. The three of us had great laughs over the years. Esther brought me around to meet all the customers and that was a memorable experience! My dairy farming background meant that I was used to working irregular hours. You were never finished on a farm and it is the same with the bakery. Having occasionally worked in the bakery, I have found baking to be a most satisfying occupation – it is the ideal combination of physical and mental work.

Because it's a service business, you have to ensure that there is a minimum of breakdowns with machinery. John Lucas was a fitter with a phenomenal brain and ability. The bigger the problem the better for him! In the middle of one night a crucial bolt on one of the machines broke. He went to his treasure trove of a van and came in with a screwdriver which he broke up and created a bolt to keep the machine going for the night. Arthur Butler was another amazing man. He could make any piece of equipment to suit our needs. A blacksmith by profession, Arthur welded and designed many useful items which made life in the bakery easier.

I always said that Esther deserves great credit for what she has achieved. She inherited a demanding business and developed it so successfully, including adding a coffee shop business. It was part and parcel of her life and it was a very challenging one. The bakery trade is predominantly a man's world and it is a great tribute to Esther that she succeeded where many others failed. We both share similar philosophies and we are interested in a project using organically grown local wheat for our bread. It's a lofty ambition, but a biodynamic grain has been bred in Switzerland which is good for growing in our climate and we are looking for a miller to advance the possibilities of having locally grown, organic flour for our bakery. There is great satisfaction being involved in an activity and work that you believe in. The eighteen years here have gone so quickly and, looking back, I must say that Co. Waterford has been very good to me!

John Barron
(Joe and Joan Barron's nephew)

My grandfather John started the bakery in 1887 and also had Harrington's Hotel in Cappoquin. When he died, my father Jack inherited it. He married May Daly from Lismore who had been born in 1910, but had a short life, dying in 1938. Not long after, the hotel and bakery went downhill and his brother Joe took it over and brought the bakery back to its former glory. Not without the considerable help of his five daughters: Deirdre, Esther, Margo, Noreen and Siobhan. I was born in 1936, and as my mother died in 1938 I didn't grow up in the bakery. I have fond memories of going out in the van with my uncle Joe. It was fantastic meeting the customers. Uncle Joe knew everyone. I don't know how we got around to deliver everyone's bread as we were offered tea in almost every house. He would say, 'This is Jack's son', and I'd feel proud. The Baby Ford 7 van was great fun. Even though I was a diabetic, I went for the sweet things. I loved the cakes and now when I go to the bakery, the smells are just gorgeous. I'm now based in Newcastle under Lyme, and I think of Cappoquin as the engine room of a ship, while nearby Lismore is more like the VIP Lounge.

Noreen Cormican
(Joe and Joan Barron's daughter)

I was the eldest of the five daughters and while I chose not to be any more involved than I had to be, living over the bakery meant I performed my share of family chores. This included helping with unloading and cleaning out the bread van, taking the bread from the bakery in a cart where it could cool before being arranged on the shop shelves. There was no question of not helping, and the five of us sisters would watch each other, making sure one wasn't doing less than the other. I remember the gentle hum of the oven. The occasional time when the noise stopped meant something was wrong. The house had a certain rhythm all of its own. Daddy got up to be well and ready for the 5am start. He wasn't a great sleeper so when he went to bed at 9pm, the household became quiet. I remember one year he went to Knock and we all went wild and stayed up making noise until 10pm. We thought it was such a treat to have the freedom of the extra hour up.

My most vivid frightening memory is of the Weights and Measures man. A burly, dark-blue uniformed man complete with cap, he would arrive and randomly weigh the loaves to check they were not being sold under weight. We would hear he was in town and somehow he struck fear in us. We were never found to have underweight loaves but we were always happy when he left. Our parents never spoke about him in front of us, but we'd pick up that he wasn't welcome.

I didn't relish working behind the counter of the shop either, worrying about muddling amounts and giving the right change. It just wasn't my calling. Instead I became a nurse. However, I look back on those days with great joy and nostalgia. It was a happy time. Every time I come home to Cappoquin a friend reminds me that I have never really left it. I'd like to be involved in the bakery now, but I live in Co. Offaly and it's like being in another world to my life in Cappoquin.

41

1cwt of sugar and timber chests of tea would arrive on the train from Musgrave's in Cork. This created work to divide the sugar into 2lb thick, brown paper bags sealed with Sellotape to sell in the shop. The tea was weighed to make 1/4lb blue bags and had to be done meticulously to ensure precise amounts.

Kate Cormican
(Noreen's daughter)

As kids the constant smell throughout my grandmother's (Joan Barron's) house and the Aga in the warm kitchen were memorable when we visited from Offaly. I thought the ovens in the bakery were huge and was a little bit afraid of them. I wanted to look inside them, but not too far in. I always thought I shouldn't go too close or I might get trapped inside them, with their big heavy doors. I remember Granny keeping the butter in a cupboard as she never wanted it to be hard from the fridge. She was particular about certain things and always prepared her breakfast tray ready for the morning. She was precise and would correct us, wanting us to be mannerly, on our best behaviour at all times. I'd often hop into the bed with her and we would both listen to the transistor radio until she had her breakfast in bed. She'd be wearing her cosy woolly pink bed jacket. We'd sit there not talking, but happy as Larry.

Mark Cormican
(Noreen's son)

My mother's former home was always a hive of activity with my grandmother enjoying people coming into the kitchen for a chat. There was always a bit of craic there. There was always a sense of productivity too. I'd hear Aunty Esther coming along asking what was happening with this and that, marshalling the troops – which I understand as I work in management too. My grandmother was always elegant, you'd know she was happy, and she loved the family coming to see her. I always enjoyed the smell in the shop. I remember climbing up a ladder to get at the sweets high up. I loved Fry's Chocolate Cream and the wrapping was a little bit like Cadbury's Milk Chocolate and at the age of eight or nine I sometimes mistook one for the other so I would climb back up for the Fry's and get caught by Esther. In the bakery you could smell history. The ovens were fascinating: the long peels were like long-handled shovels for reaching into the ovens to get the bread out and you could feel the heat on your face when the doors were open. When we stayed overnight, as we lived in the Midlands, you would hear the ovens hum at 5am and you'd know that some industrial work was going on down below while you had a lie in for another few hours. When we had a mobile home in Ardmore, Granny would visit us and always brought a box of buns and things like Battenbergs. I still love the Chester cake. I reckon the cost/profit was not greatly balanced. They use such good quality ingredients you'd imagine it wouldn't pay them.

Margo Murphy
(Joe and Joan Barron's daughter)

I trained for four years as a confectioner in the Kylemore, Dublin and then in Phelan's Bakery in Broad Street, Waterford. I was paid thirty shillings a week in the first year in Dublin. It was a wonderful experience. I had no money to spare so I joined the Legion of Mary which had nine guilds around the city and provided me with plenty of inexpensive social activities. I loved dancing, but there was no drink involved so I was quite safe! My apprenticeship started with making brown and white soda bread, then I graduated onto light bracks, scones, queen cakes, custard slices, fresh cream sponges, éclairs, then large doughnuts.

I brought the skills for these favourites home as bread was enough for Daddy to cope with and he didn't have time to make confectionery. I'd just make some of the cakes at weekends. Daddy had a big book on cakes and he'd study them. He liked to make rock buns, scones, Madeira cake, and our Chester cake was well known. It was made with leftover bread, fruit and spices and was always available along with the bread. I remember a customer who brought the sultana cake from our bakery to the Macra Field Day competition and won first prize. No-one seemed to mind, not even Daddy. I was annoyed but couldn't say a word. Daddy called customers his friends. We were brought up not to talk about anyone.

We didn't discuss politics at table and I didn't even know what party Daddy was in. One way people tried to find out who you supported was to ask what newspaper you read. The *Press* was associated with Fianna Fáil, the *Irish Independent* with Fine Gael. When we were asked, we always said both the *Irish Independent* and the *Press*, and the *Cork Examiner*! 'Be modest; be humble,' Daddy used to say. It was also considered impolite to talk about money so that was a topic avoided too.

I had great sympathy for Daddy, with no son to help him traditionally, so he had to depend on his daughters. We were brought up with hard work and long hours, but the business supplied us with our bread and butter so we got on with it. I wanted to be a hairdresser. I'm a home bird and didn't want to leave for training. I stayed a while but I was never forced to do anything by my parents. Daddy was one of twelve and had wanted to be a journalist, but his father had no-one to help him so he gave up his dream. I think he made sure none of us was forced to do anything we didn't want to do.

Willie McGrath drove vans for years and was a great help to Daddy. We grew up with him and he was very much part of our lives. The rule of the time was no meat on a Friday, but he would say, 'I think it's a Good Friday when you get a bit of meat.' At the age of sixteen I'd pick him up from his house on a Friday and could smell the steak and onions. We couldn't tell anyone at home about it as to us it was a mortal sin.

The convent took lots of bread, and we would deliver to them after school. There was also an industrial school in Cappoquin and, with one hundred boys, they bought a lot of bread. They always took the double length pan loaf. On Saturdays shops might ask us to send more to them. We had to react quickly to consumer demand.

Mammy was a kind woman, a great cook who never raised her voice – a real lady. She lived to be ninety-three and it was only in her last year that she became frail. We always ate healthy food. She was like a nurse to everyone. We had boiled pearl barley and got regular worm doses in the form of chocolate sweets – it seemed to be fashionable in those days. She was a grounded person, cool, calm and collected; stern, but positive about right and wrong. Her father Andrew Hickey was the first peace commissioner in Lismore.

The ovens were turned on each Christmas Day and people brought their turkeys. I loved the smell of the turkeys roasting with their delicious stuffing. We had to call to the houses, about twelve of them, to tell them when they were ready. Daddy often got up on St Stephen's Day to bake if people ran out of bread.

We went to Ardmore every Saturday in the summer and Clonea on many Thursdays and had picnics in the Knockmealdowns and we also went to Stradbally Cove where Daddy had a sister married.

43

If they can make penicillin out of mouldy bread

RON

they can sure make something out of you

MUHAMMAD ALI

John Murphy
(Margo's son)

I always linked my grandparents' bakery and Cappoquin together and there was an air of wonder and awe even though it was only sixty miles away from us in south Kilkenny. Coming in the Dungarvan road, with the stone walls, sweeping around the bend, was a beautiful journey, full of anticipation. Even before we left home there would be differences. My father would check the oil and water in the car, as if for a very long journey. He would always put on a suit for a visit. Then when we arrived there for, say, Sunday lunch, we would be fed first and then allowed to play in the bakery. I remember the green door ajar. If it was a bright day shafts of sun would stream in and highlight what I think was a slight sheen of flour everywhere, a cloudy hue contrasting with the dark timber loft. It was quite heavenly. It reminded me a bit of *Oliver Twist* – a look back in time. On Sundays there was a beautiful silence and the ovens would have cooled down.

It was different when we went there on a week's holidays. We might arrive at lunchtime of the working week when the bakers would be finishing up. We would run to Grandad Joe who would be standing by the table in the bakery. He looked huge to us in his white t-shirt and pants. I always felt he was very happy to see me and my brother Joe. He would offer us 10p if we would rub our faces on his day's facial stubble. It was like a test to see if we could take a bit of hardship.

The bakery was a wonderful place for me. I would climb up to the loft where the bags of flour were, and could see the hopper and funnel through which the flour dropped. When I got older I was delighted to get a job stacking the cooked loaves onto trays. We used double thickness of sacks on our hands as heat-resisters (you wouldn't be allowed that these days with health and safety regulations). You had to learn how to catch the loaves from the baker who tipped them out of the tins, four at a time. It was very easy to burn your arms. You had to move fast, you didn't want to be a slow cog in the wheel. You really had to concentrate. The old machine for slicing the bread would make a rat-tat-tat sound. Aunt Siobhan made it look easy, but you could easily cut your fingers so we weren't allowed near it.

I would sleep over the bakery and wake to the hum of the ovens. Sometimes I went in the van with Milo Murray. We would go to families where boxes were left at the end of their lanes with a list of what was needed. We left their groceries and bread. It was all done on trust.

There was an apparition in nearby Mount Melleray around the same time as in Ballinspittle. My cousin Páraic McCarthy and I were run off our feet in the shop keeping up with the demand for cakes. We were snowed under with work. I remember the black and white tiles on the serving side of the counter worn down to the last from years of work.

Later in the 1980s when I was in my late teens I was more interested in the girls working in the bakery. I was green as grass, but it gave my time in the bakery an added dimension. Another memory I have of Cappoquin is Collender's pub, a few doors down from the bakery. The window advertisement for Babycham, with its little deer, fading over the years, was one of my landmarks. If I ever thought I was lost, I could head for that window, but I never went in the door. To me the whole scene was like something from Maeve Binchy's *Circle of Friends* – a step back in time in Ireland.

46

Laura Murphy
(Margo's daughter)

I spent a few weeks working in the coffee shop in my mid-teens. I remember my grandfather's walking stick and his chair in the corner where he would sit and he always gave me ten or twenty pence to get an ice-cream across the road in Meskills. Granny was quiet, but got things done. She was industrious, but in a quiet way. She would pop her head into the shop to see if there was anyone she would like to greet. A mark of growing up for me was being able to fit into Granny's shoes. She was a nice lady, I was fond of her. I always joked with my mother that Granny and Aunty Esther gave us our finishing touches, our best manners, the right words – Granny was a lady to her finger-tips. I noticed she was eyeing up my then-boyfriend Tom when I brought him to meet her. She was keen for us to get engaged (even sooner than we were). When we finally did and planned an October wedding, she said I would need sleeves in my dress. And I did get elbow length sleeves! I'm proud of where my mother came from, the bakery. Not every-one has a bakery in the family. The ovens were a wonder. The bread sat on trolleys to cool; the place was full of buzz, buzz, buzz. They all worked very hard. I remember the heat of the bakery, as a child it seemed very hot. And the big timber paddles.

Joe Murphy
(Margo's son)

Between visiting on holidays and working I had good fun in my Aunt Esther's bakery and my mother's childhood home. As a child I thought of the bakery as full of mechanical marvels. There was a big trailer that would hold the bread and take it to the bread slicer. This was where I would stand and watch for warm bits of crusty bread to fall off the machine. It was the best instant toast ever. I would fill myself with it.

I was and still am in awe of the bakers who are so strong and have their own techniques and character. Handling the peel, filling spaces to the best advantage and getting the loaves in so they would cook at the same time, near and far away from the walls of the oven, was all very tricky. They all had their own way of moulding and handling the dough, and I had the privilege of working with some of them and learning how to do it all. It was very hard work, but I was used to that growing up on a farm. In fact, I'd say it takes similar physical strength to farming. It was all quite tricky and a lot could go wrong. Esther would get cross if it wasn't all perfect, and some of it might have to be made into breadcrumbs or used some way of another if it wasn't good enough to go on the shelves. The people working there operated as a unit and the radio was on loud to keep us all awake. The worst part was the clean-up afterwards.

You'd be getting tired, especially in the heat, and the whole place would have to be done. The dough seemed to latch on to the aluminium parts of the machines and was a shocker to get off. Even though there are many stages of making bread well, the most interesting thing to me in many ways is that it's a simple process which ends up as a nice product at the end of the day.

47

Siobhan McCarthy
(Joe and Joan Barron's daughter)

As I got older, I liked being in the shop, going to the bank, dealing with turnover tax, doing the stock and having things ready for the auditors – all the financial affairs of the business. But that didn't mean I was excused from the physical work. I also had to unload bread and count loaves into the vehicle. When my father bought eggs from local farms on his rounds, I counted them too. I spent time on the road with him aged nine to twelve. On Wednesdays there was a longer route as far as Clonmel. We'd have a flask of tea to have with our sandwiches. I loved that exclusive time with him. My happiest memory was being out with Daddy in the van. I even liked going to mass with him. We were used to early mornings, so 6am mass was not such a hardship, but we were tired by 9pm. It was a get-on-with-it lifestyle.

It was all about knowing what customers liked. Some liked bread fresh out of the oven, others, like me, preferred it a day old. The creamery at the top of the town was a busy place. People came with horses and carts to deliver their milk and there would be lots of bread needed. They would queue at the co-op for vegetables and meat. Jim Nugent was employed by the co-op, and he would fill a chest with thirty loaves from us as many as three times during the course of the day.

In exchange we bought Knockmeal butter in a sort of contra-deal. Monday to Saturday that was the routine, selling bread to the co-op and buying their supplies. I remember the co-op money system with its pulley. You put your money in a brass container which was pulled along overhead to the office where they would take our money out and replace it with change. It was slow but we were always intrigued with it as kids.

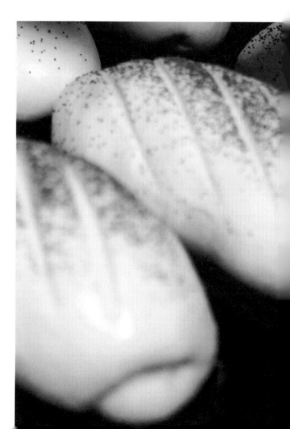

Denise McCarthy
(Siobhan's daughter)

When I was small I loved going to visit Granny Joan as that meant we would get to have a snoop around the bakery when it was closed at night time and weekends. When I was very small I thought the bakery was a very scary place, the men in their white uniforms and aprons, the big, noisy machinery, the fire and the brick ovens which were so big. I imagined that you could get locked in there, as they were so big you could fit almost eight people in them. There was a sliding door into the bakery which was difficult to open and close and I would be afraid I would get locked in the room. On weekdays I was amazed at all the activity, the noisy machinery, and wished I could make the things the staff were making. They were so nice and friendly.

When I was older I worked there a lot in the coffee shop and the bread shop, and Granny would always look after me. If I hadn't my lunch by a certain time (if it was busy) she would come looking for me. She would want me to have little breaks and chat with her. Whilst she did look after the staff there, I felt I always got that extra special treatment.

Often in the shop customers would recognise that there was somebody new serving in the shop, and they would say, 'Well, you are definitely a Barron anyway; which of the Barron sisters is your mother?' Eventually I would get to know the customers and barely needed to ask what they wanted to buy as it would almost be the same each day. Some customers would want to feel the bread before buying it, often coming in behind the counter to examine it. Some customers would be passing through and living up the country and they would stock up and buy a lot of bread. It was very obvious the different preferences customers had: there was one customer in particular who wanted the crust of the pan burnt and you would have to pick out the darkest crust for him, then others would like a lightly cooked pan. Some customers had a daily order and you would put it aside under the counter as often the bread would be sold out by the evening time.

There were times after a long, busy day when you would have everything put away and the doors shut and someone would ring the doorbell looking for bread. Others, maybe at work until late, arranged to call after closing hours. By the end of the day you would be wrecked – being on your feet from 8.30am to 6pm each day was tiring. Then Granny would want you to sit down and tell her about the day, who was in and how busy it had been.

Barbara McCarthy
(Siobhan's daughter)

The smell of the bread as it came out of the ovens was my first memory of my grandparents' bakery. It was put into an old-fashioned cart to get it to the slicer. We used to take little fragments, encouraging little extra bits to stick out so we could pull at them. They were fresh and hot and we had to dodge Aunty Esther as we did it. I loved watching the old-fashioned way of kneading bread. I remember the huge, shiny bowl and an enormous dough hook, and it made a noise like horses' hooves clicking. The people who worked there were special, particularly Milo and Paddy Murray. We thought the confectionery was wonderful as my mother didn't allow this kind of treat at home. I worked in the coffee shop from time to time when needed and couldn't believe I could have whatever I wanted. Grandmother Joan would be there and always had a word for us. I remember the tray of Chester cakes and apple tarts on the counter and the bread piled up. There was a chest with chocolate and loose sweets. On occasions when Esther went on holiday my mother would run the bakery and it was always an anxious time as the timings were so important and lots could go wrong.

Páraic McCarthy
(Siobhan's son)

I can still see my Grandfather Joe working, with his walking stick hanging on the table while he was kneading. The bread would come out hot on the trolley and the gloves they used were square like sacks, woollen and brown. The pans would be in trays with a top like a lid for the sliced bread so they would be even on top. Lovely, hot smells, different bread to any other I have tasted. I never worked there, despite being only five miles away. I slept the odd night in a room over where the van would come and go noisily. That's where the slicing machine was which was noisy too. Because he had arthritis, Grandad would be in bed and would give us ten pence to spend. He was a swimmer, and we'd go to the beach in Ardmore in the Passat and he would listen to a match in the car. He said the seawater was good for us with the iodine. Granny Joan always went for a nap. When Grandad passed away she became busy with friends and the Widows' Association.

No more turkey
but I'd like some more of the bread it ate.

HANK KETCHAM

Deirdre Hallahan
(Joe and Joan Barron's daughter)

I worked in the bakery as a confectioner, but I wasn't committed to the job – I was easily diverted! I'd say Dad was disappointed when I left. My husband Percy rallied when needed and made bread with Margo in emergencies. The fresh cream for the confectionery came from the creamery. I used to go with a jug and fill it up for home and then later for the confectionery. Dad loved making gingerbread. I followed in Dad's footsteps and am involved in Lismore choir. We were always doing something. Drink was not a big feature of our house. Uncle Hugh, my father's brother, came when Dad was ill. He had his own bakery in Dublin and had worked in Boland's. He retired and then became available to help Daddy. One Shrove Tuesday he set up a Primus stove and made and sold pancakes in the bakery.

Sunday lunch was Mum and Dad's treat. We loved Arbutus Lodge in Cork, the food, the service. My parents never got used to the idea of queuing for food. I also remember Mrs O'Sullivan's lovely, clean, farmer's butter which we always enjoyed. She'd bring us in for Spotted Dog cake and tea. 'Listen child,' she'd say. She always made goodie (bread and milk) for us.

I worked as a receptionist in the Imperial Hotel in Cork and at Eccles Hotel, Glengarrif. I also worked in the bakery on and off and, like the swallows, came and went. I like meeting people and the bakery was confining, but I loved icing the queen cakes. The flour men would deliver after 6pm which we considered late. I might have had a date but had to stay on as my father insisted on giving them something to eat. They may have kept us until last knowing that they would get a good feed. One night I said I heard a man drunk and singing. To protect him Dad said I dreamed it. He never wanted to show people up and instead preferred to see the best side of people. Anything for a quiet life. Out in the country if people tried to cheat him, he let them. He just smiled. One man came after Dad died and said that Daddy had given him tea and sugar when he had no money. I think Dad felt part of the community; it wasn't about making money. He worked hard for us and was able to provide for us so we felt we were never short of anything. If I needed money I was allowed to go to the till for it. A good education for us was important to both my parents. That's why we were sent off to boarding school in Loreto, Waterford. My mother had gone to the Ursulines in Blackrock, Cork. She was a lovely cook – egg custard and her marmalade pudding were specialities. When Daddy was ill, she was great at making egg flips for him and he loved tripe and onions. 'It's as natural to die as it is to be born,' he said as he became ill.

51

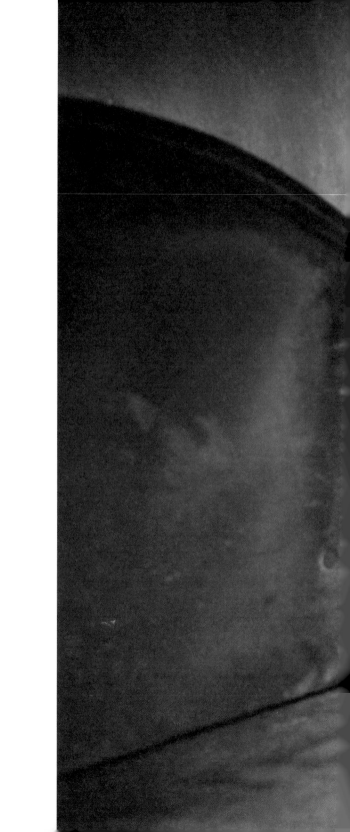

FLOUR AUGOR 2 BULK FLOUR COMPRESSOR

52

54

Emma Hallahan
(Deirdre's daughter)

Every happy childhood memory I have, Granny Joan is in it. While I was in junior school my cousin Denise and I stayed with her every Friday so I could go to music lessons in the morning. She made stew for me every Saturday after my lesson and couldn't understand why I didn't like jelly! Even though the café was there, I was always in the home kitchen where people who worked in the shop and bakery came and went, which I thought was lovely. I remember Miriam Cunningham in the shop and I would help her to make up the boxes for the cakes. There were plenty of shelves for storage. I also helped make doughnuts and éclairs and I loved making ice-cream in the summer with strawberries. I was delighted with the big jars of sweets which we were never allowed at home. We would take a selection of bullseyes and other forbidden hard sweets in a bag. Joan Ormonde (Cahillane) was the confectioner there when I had my thirteenth birthday. Each year I was allowed to pick whatever cake I wanted. This time I wanted a sponge in the shape of the number thirteen, so somehow Joan found the baking tin shapes and I had the best cake ever, and have a photograph to prove it.

Owen Hallahan
(Deirdre's son)

My sister, myself and a friend from Scouts would visit Granny. She would always allow us to go to the shop to take a bun each. Our trick was to eat one of each of the different types of cakes while we were in the shop. Then we'd put a cake each for us on a plate and bring them to the kitchen to have with Granny. We would also fill up on soft drinks which came from a set of taps in the shop, so we'd be well satisfied by the time we had finished in the shop. I did a week or two in the bakery about eight years ago when I was about twenty-six. The heat was wicked. Rolling the dough, putting it into tins, loading the trolley was my job and generally giving a hand. It was a great lesson, great to see it all happening and it's great to see the ovens are still being used the traditional way. My grandmother was a great woman, she'd tell you straight, but she let you work away.

Michael Barron-Wike
(Hugh (Pat) Barron's son)

It was 1979 when I finally made it to my father's hometown of Cappoquin. My parents had emigrated to the US from Canada via England back in the 1940s during the Second World War. My father was born in Swansea, Wales, to his Irish father, James Stanislaus Barron and his English/Welsh mother, Flora Hancock. My grandmother died when my father was only two, so my grandfather remarried a Welsh woman who was a teacher and lived in Bishopston on the Gower Peninsula. Both my father and aunt Nora were sent off to school each year, my father to Cappoquin/Dungarvan.

Soon after the war, my parents divorced. This was why I was all the more pleased to be with Esther and her family after so many years of not being connected. Unfortunately Joe had taken sick and was in hospital in Cork, so Esther and her mother, Aunt Joan, were running the bakery. Aunt Joan immediately endeared herself to me with her quiet demeanour and kind smile. My first morning in the Barron house on the Square was a memorable one. As I awoke at 5am, the entire bedroom was enveloped with a rich, robust aroma. I quickly got dressed and ran downstairs to inspect the loaves myself. There was Esther and her staff in the dim light of the morning, sliding the browned loaves of bread out of those old brick ovens. The baskets of baked, steaming loaves were wheeled away and packaged for the van deliveries that morning. Naturally I enquired if the bakers needed an 'impartial taste tester' for that particular order. Esther and her staff laughed and handed me a warm loaf. That crust so crisp, the centre so soft. And the melting butter that somehow found its way onto my slices. Aunt Joan's homemade jam only enhanced the experience further. I was able to meet Uncle Joe briefly in hospital in Cork. He focused on me intently and I could see the earnestness of his character. It was clear that Esther had inherited his passion for the business. Now, as a fourth generation baker with a business plan, she had established goals to fundamentally improve the bakery. Her education at college provided her with the tools to take this business into the twenty-first century. I could see the changes beginning to happen back then for Esther, and I could feel the excitement of its pending success in the air. It was the beginning of a new era for the Barron bakery.

55

John Power
(Nicholas and Nora Power 's (Coffey) son)

My mother was the daughter of Margaret Susan Barron who was a daughter of John and Hanora which made Joe Barron my grand-uncle. In the 1960s I worked in the bakery for three years and often went back to give a hand when needed. I started as a sort of apprentice with Joe and stayed in the house during the week as I lived too far away in Stradbally, and got the huge sum of £6 a week. I was able to buy a push bike with two weeks' wages and I did just that so I could cycle home at weekends. In those days there wasn't much equipment and everything was done by hand. Big lumps of dough had to be lifted on to the table from the huge bowls. Then, if you didn't work quickly enough or took your eye off it, the yeast would work in the dough and expand it too much and it would drip off the table on to the floor. This would be even more likely to happen during the summer, especially if it was hot outside. It would affect all the timings of the operation. We had to play catch up with the yeast, working at a mad pace. You would be working in one part of the bakery and you'd look around and it would look like the proving bread was boiling over. We would have to get our skids on to cut up the bread dough.

Joe's brown bread was superb. There were big troughs like you would use for feeding pigs. Joe would keep the dough there and would take a few handfuls and add it to the next batch, like the original sourdough method. Joe reckoned it added body to the bread and I noticed it gave it a shine too. Joe always put the best of ingredients into his produce. He got the best farmer's butter and put it into the bracks along with eggs straight from the farms.

As Joe become ill and a bit bothered he still came into the bakery. One night he came in and put a handful of whitewash into the mix instead of one of the ingredients that looked the same. I don't know why it was close by. The dough went yellow so it was obvious something was wrong. Poor Joe was disgusted with himself. He was always so careful and this was a sure sign to him that he could make mistakes and needed to keep out of the bakery. He had always been the first up and was always ahead of me in the bakery, making the first batch of dough and heating up the ovens. We needed strong arms to lift the dough from the long troughs. Even though there were mixers at that stage, we still had to cut it up and leave it to rest and prove. The ovens made all the difference to the taste of the bread. That very hot oven, cooling once the bread went in, was the secret. We would add some water to the oven to help the sliced bread to stay softer than the crusty loaves. Joe was a perfectionist, and was always looking to innovate and keep up with the times. Joe would sit down and have anything left over from tea the previous evening and that could include tripe or cabbage. He had an amazing constitution. I'd have to look away.

I used to walk to mass with my grandmother and Aunty Hess who really thought she was a young one. I made the mistake one day of telling her she was *like* a young one. I was told that was an insult as she thought she *was* a young one. I think Hessie had a fear of hard times. She had gone through the war, with rationing and general hardship and she wanted to be sure that didn't happen again. I remember delivering with Uncle Joe during the war and leaving supplies at gates and people would settle up later. Some of them didn't settle up until after the war, but at least they did eventually. I must say that it was the smaller, humbler cottage dwellers who did pay up. Some of the big house owners didn't bother to pay their debts at all. 'The harm of the day go with it,' Joe used to say. He thought it wasn't worth worrying about, and he himself would never get a loan for anything. He said that you shouldn't have it if you couldn't pay for it. He preferred peace of mind – a lesson for today!

I was only about four at the time of the war, but I remember Joe buying wheat from farmers and bringing it to my father's crusher. We had our own electricity supply and were able to crush the wheat so Uncle Joe could add it to the flour rations he got. Somehow the bread still seemed quite black to me and I don't think there was much gluten in it to help it to rise, but it was edible and we were glad of it.

Kevin Barron
(Hugh Barron's son)

The bricks at the front of the oven in Barron's Bakery came from Garranturton, near Williamstown in the parish of Stradbally. There were two old derelict houses and one of them had the bricks which were recycled for use in the bakery. I also remember the ration books during the war. We were fortunate as on a farm we always had something to eat. We grew our own vegetables and we could kill a pig. I remember that tea and petrol were rationed. Petrol was 1/6d a gallon then. Farmers got tokens and would swap them for what they needed more. I'm long retired now but I still make brown loaves at home for the family.

I was travelling through Europe on a six-month 'walkabout' and had met a fellow Canadian in a youth hostel outside Lisbon. Lisbon had experienced a flood, so no trains were able to go in or out, and the nearest hostel was in a town just east of Lisbon. Everyone else in the hostel was Portuguese, so Willy and I had dinner together, and ultimately ended up travelling together, first to Spain and Italy, then to Greece. It was on a beach in Greece that we decided to go to Ireland, purely by chance. Willy asked if I wanted an English or an Irish Breakfast. I chose Irish, which began a discussion about the fact that while I had family in Ireland, I had never actually been there.

When I arrived at the bakery, unannounced, complete with backpack and friend in tow (and probably more than a little dishevelled), I was greeted like a long lost son. Since Cappoquin is tiny, it was not hard to find the bakery, so we walked in and I said to the person at the counter, 'Hello, I'm Kevin Barron.' A little confused, they went to get Esther, my cousin. Esther said something like. 'Oh my gosh, you're Hugh's son?' She immediately went to get her mother, Joan, who welcomed me like her own son. In turn, someone was sent to get Uncle Joe (who was actually my great uncle), and from there we were embraced into the family in what seemed like a continuous group hug.

Walking into the bakery for the first time was an amazing experience. Not only was this a rediscovery of my family heritage but every molecule of the bakery was infused with the heavenly scent of what seemed to be the aromatic equivalent of manna from heaven. I swear that even if the ovens were shut down and all the bread and pastries were removed, the bakery itself emanated such powerful aromas that the effect would continue for years. Remarkably though, there was not the sense of suffocation that many restaurants and some bakeries suffer from. The air was fresh and felt like a summer breeze. At work I could see Joe's hands which were the most amazing thing to behold: large and strong, but beautifully veined and articulated.

57

Margaret Daly
(Peadar Hickey's daughter)

I grew up in Lismore and Joan Barron was my aunt and my father's only sister. My mother died young when I was twenty-one and I was brought into the Barron family like a sixth sister, staying every weekend. We always enjoyed Barron's bread, but we also enjoyed seeing the Thompson's van arrive on Thursdays at 4pm with their cakes. It meant we had delicious, fresh bread delivered by Barron's every day and an extra treat towards the end of the week. Aunty Hess knew everything and everybody and when my mother went to Cappoquin to have her hair done every Friday, Hess would look after me and give me a bottle of Jennings' lemonade. I was really impressed by Aunt Joan as she had been brought up having everything done for her, but wasn't afraid to throw herself into hard work in the bakery when she got married. She was seen more in the background and had a quiet presence, but she was strong. She always said, 'Don't forget the core business is bread. People will always want bread.' She was great for advice, and people often went to her with all sorts of problems. I greatly admired how the whole family worked so well together. One of my most vivid memories is of knowing the seasons by Barron's display window. We knew all the occasions were coming – Valentine's Day, Mother's Day, Easter, Christmas. I also remember Uncle Michael Barron helping out in summer time. He would only eat the bread stale. He thought that fresh bread was bad for him, so his would be set aside in a special place until it was just right for him. Nowadays I buy it sliced and freeze half in bags so I always have some to hand.

Jane Barron
(Hubert Barron's daughter)

My father Hubert and Joe Barron were brothers and we always say that it was my father who was responsible for Uncle Joe and Aunty Joan getting married as he looked after the bakery while they went on honeymoon. They came up here to Dublin after the wedding and I remember Aunty Joan showing me the pair of shoes she bought. She was very particular about shoes as they had to be stylish as well as comfortable. Dad went down to the bakery during the war to help out as it was so difficult to get staff. I remember him being away during the week and coming back at weekends.

Miriam Barron
(Jack Barron's daughter)

I grew up with my grandparents on Main Street in Cappoquin. I used to play with Margo and Noreen in the loft of the bakery where the flour was kept and well remember looking down at Uncle Joe as he kneaded the dough. In the summer he would bring us to Whiting Bay for a swim; he was the kindest, gentlest man. Aunt Joan was a lady to her fingertips. I was a bit wild and Aunt Hessie would keep me in check, but I channelled it through Irish dancing and drama which were a big part of life in the town. I ended up as stage door keeper in the Fortune Theatre, Covent Garden, London until I retired seven years ago. I got to meet stars such as Joe Fiennes who was gorgeous! I live in London now and have fond memories of the easy welcome I always got in people's homes in Cappoquin. Religion is important to me and I got that from growing up in Cappoquin. We were never indoctrinated, as some people suggest. Saying the rosary was a part of life in the Barron household which was comforting and enjoyable, as it is now. I'm a happier person for it.

59

Earning a Crust Memories from Staff Members

Paddy 'Baker' Murray My first encounter with Barron's was getting bread for my mother at the age of twelve or thirteen. Esther's Aunt Hessie then got me to collect yeast from the railway station which led to other after-school odd jobs such as greasing tins. We didn't all get to third level education in those days. Cappoquin Bacon Factory was an option, so when I think about it, I consider myself lucky to have been in a bakery and later worked there full-time. The hours were unsociable though, going to bed when others were going out. I went in at 5am and worked to 12 or 1pm – it was long enough. Eventually I could do everything on my own, and did in the end. We always had mixing machines, they were mechanical but not automated, so we still had to use our own judgement. We would weigh one in every ten lots of dough, to check. It was hot, especially in summer, but we got acclimatised.

I was with Joe for a good number of years and learned everything from him. He knew it all inside out – everything. I was always learning from him. We would work away quietly together. There was no shouting, you just followed Joe and learned from him. Each oven would be ninety per cent full most of the time and we would half-fill the oven at other times with bracks. The skill was checking the temperature gauge and to know from one batch to the next when it was right to put the loaf dough in. We used a timber peel [a long-handled shovel] to fill the oven. The temperature was 600 to 650 degrees Fahrenheit and the reducing heat would bake the bread. Once the bread was cooked, the heat falling further would be perfect for the cakes.

I got satisfaction from doing a good job for the people of the town, like Joe Barron did. We got a great crust on the bread and I still enjoy it toasted with marmalade. All those modern improvers used in commercially produced bread give it a texture I don't like. I could never eat it. By 1986/7 I was tired and retired. These days I don't miss getting up early.

Milo Murray Having worked part-time in the bakery from a young age, I continued to work there for another fifteen years as a part-time van driver; the rest of my time was spent on the family farm. Joe Barron was hardworking. There would be himself and one or two of us and we were kept going all night. At bank holidays we worked even harder as there was extra bread to be made. We just got on with it, didn't think of it as hard work or soft. For me it was more comfortable than being out in the cold with the cows. Inside it was warm and was never too hot for me, though Joe would always make sure we young fellas were kept away from the oven door.

63

Denis Murray I started working at the bakery at the age of thirteen, helping out after school, cleaning up after my brothers Pat and Milo who worked there full time. Greasing tins was one occupation, perfectly timed for after school and in preparation for the next day's baking with Joe Barron. Mrs Barron always gave me something to eat when I arrived, and I was glad of it after the long day at school. I would do an hour and twenty minutes work before going home. I'd do a half-day on Saturday, and at thirteen years of age, I'd do whatever needed to be done as quickly as possible to earn my money and get out to have fun.

A Jack-of-All-Trades, I learned a lot about baking as the years went by. I learned that if the oven was completely filled with bread, the bread wasn't quite as crusty, so I preferred the result of when the oven was only three-quarters filled. I love a good crusty bread, not black, but crispy. Barron's people like their bread crusty. My family had a farm and I often got up at 8.30am to feed the cattle, drove for the day in the day job, came back, fed cattle and at 7.15pm went to the bakery to work until 4.30am. Baking is a nice job, fulfilling, but there are no shortcuts. You have to be there for every stage and be sharp so you get the timings right. At 8pm you would get going with the ovens, mixing maybe a tea brack and getting it into the oven with other bits and pieces, and then you would have to prepare the next mix. You'd close the door of the oven, go to the mixer, divide the mix into batches, into tins, watching all the time that nothing was in the oven for too long. There was so much to do you wouldn't get a break for six hours. And you were on your feet all that time. There wasn't anybody stopping you from taking a break, it was just the demands of each of the processes. You'd never be idle!

There was great satisfaction in the job, you felt you had achieved something at the end of the morning's work. It got very hot at times and we got quite a few colds as you'd be hot and then go outside into the cold. The smells were lovely, you'd drive into the town and the gentle aromas would greet you. I loved old Joe. He had respect for what we did and I always got on well with him. I often worked with him on St Stephen's Day, baking a few batches so regular customers would have a fresh loaf. He'd be up especially early to light the ovens. I was never tempted to be a full-time baker. The hours were unsociable. Bakery people are not day people and the dust of the flour didn't suit my chest problems. It's important to have a bakery in a town. When I see the pale sliced pans you have to toast to give it taste, I say we are lucky to have a bakery in the town.

Dermot Dee In response to an ad in the local paper, in 1989 I joined Barron's as a trainee baker. I did five years, left and joined a company closer to home in Dungarvan. Then that company closed and Esther was on to me days later to offer my job back. I did another five years and loved it.

In those days we started at 4am to have it all delivered by lunchtime. Now shops want it sooner and when I went back we started at 8pm. I liked being my own boss. Once I was trained in, I worked alone and would have a few lads in from time to time to help me. It was constant work, but the time passed quickly. Esther was running the show, her father Joe was gone, but Mrs Barron would come in with tea and buns for me. I was taught a great work ethic. Getting the first batch in the ovens was crucial. I didn't mind the heat. It could be 140 degrees Fahrenheit with the two ovens on. In summer there was extra heat. It was a completely satisfying job, and I would happily return to it.

As it progressed we were introduced to more health bread etc, but I loved the brack which was baked once a week. That was my favourite. Over the years Esther would buy tins and equipment from bakers that were closing down. There was a kind of convention of selling to others and they were glad to get something for the tins which are so durable. When the reach of the bakery went as far as Dungarvan, people I knew would come up to me and tell me how much they liked the bread I baked. I enjoyed that. It had a unique taste and I was proud of it. People would often pop in to see the ovens as they are so special. The odd time that equipment went wrong we would call John Lucas who was God to us at the time as he could fix anything mechanical. Later Esther got fancy and started wrapping Christmas puddings in paper and ribbon. It was an added bonus to have the coffee shop so I could have a nice cup of tea and leftover cake. I think it's a phenomenal achievement for it still to be there.

Joan Cahillane I was a confectioner at Barron's for eleven years and left only to rear my children. I trained and worked there for four years in the shop before spending a year in America. When I came back I got going on the confectionery with Esther who taught me. I stayed with it because I liked it. It was a very busy time. We started at 6.30 in the morning and were kept going until we stopped at 4.30 in the afternoon. We were on our feet all the time as we just had to be. When I went on holidays my feet would relax and then when I got back working I'd have to put my feet in a basin of hot water after work. Then I'd get used to it again. If she saw you were off form on a day Mrs Barron would make soup for you and made you sit

down and relax. She couldn't have been nicer. We made everything from scratch, like the puff and flaky pastry which we made once a week or whenever we needed it. We had a roller which was a help but we still had to turn it, so I had good muscles on my arms. Then there was shortcrust pastry, and we made choux pastry and immediately piped it out and made éclairs, putting them into a very hot oven. Doughnuts were popular too. We made lots of Christmas cakes. I had already got to know all the customers who came into the café, so when I had to make cakes for their birthdays or even just for their Sunday tea, I knew what they liked. I made great friends there and still meet them a few times a year – Miriam Cunningham, Breda Walsh, Bernie Glavin (O'Rourke), Marcia Power and a few more and we all say we were glad we met working in Barron's.

John Power I worked for seven years at the bakery from 1987. It was tough work and the hours were unsociable, but it was regular work and I liked the staff. I started with Dermot Dee and the two of us would work together. It was hot and heavy work, but we didn't agonise about it and got on with it.

Miriam Cunningham I worked in the shop for seven years up to 1996. As a child I went to the bakehouse and helped Esther with making meringues, Madeira cakes and cleaning up. There was a nice atmosphere there, lovely and warm, maybe even too hot at times. It was part of life as a child, one of the nicer parts. In the shop we wore white coats and green and white aprons. In 1989 when there wasn't much happening due to the recession, I was glad of that job, my first out of school, and knew I was lucky to have got one I enjoyed so much. We were one of the families that had their Christmas turkey cooked in Barron's oven. They even cooked one for my son's confirmation.

Ann Prendergast I worked up to 2002 for six years in the coffee shop as waitress and doing some cooking. I knew every customer and felt part of the community. I was always learning there, you learn more in small places than large. Joan was lovely, a pure lady, and I had a great relationship with her. On a few occasions when Esther and Joe were away, I slept overnight to keep her company.

Marcia Power (O'Donoghue) I worked as a confectioner in Barron's for fourteen years up to 2004. Baking was and still is my first love. I had to give up when I had a baby as the hours were too unsociable, but I still help out from time to time. I trained first on Saturdays, working up to full-time. I would arrive at 6am, working alone until others arrived around 8.30. On my feet for the whole time, I had lots of responsibility. I liked all the Christmas baking, decorating cakes and making lots of plum puddings. We did a huge trade in chocolate éclairs, custard slices and doughnuts. Scones were the first to be made, then cream cakes, then swiss rolls, which all had to be ready by 9am. Then I made Madeira, porter cakes and buns, then pastries for the fridge ready for baking. I had to be well organised and made up icings for the day. Egg whites were used for meringues while the yolks were used for the pastry for apple tarts. Leftover yolks were put into the brown bread. There was no waste whatsoever. We sieved and used leftover cake crumbs for birthday cakes, and breadcrumbs were used for Chester cakes and plum puddings. I would prepare the stock for the week, getting ahead for the extra produce at the weekend. You'd get into a routine, and most of the time you knew what was needed for the week. In fact I really knew what had to be done at any time of the day. Joan was a real lady. I had lunch every day with her; she even made tea for me and looked after me like a daughter. She would give out to me if I went out in the cold without a hat. They were happy days. Two years before I left I went on the van run to Tallow. Meeting people was ok, but I preferred the warmth of the bakery.

Ray Anthony I have been the Barron's accountant since the mid-1960s just when turnover tax was introduced and before the advent of VAT. I was one of Joe's good friends and, though I supported Kilkenny, my home county, during clashes with Waterford, I enjoyed long discussions with him on hurling. I never saw a man with such an interest in his work. He was a real artisan baker with a huge interest in his craft. He never allowed his equipment to run down, was continually updating. He was old stock, but forward-looking. He had great integrity, paid promptly which was unusual enough at the time. I still love the bread, it's a great waist expander. At least it is a pleasure to eat, not like what is produced in large bakeries – water standing up! It's sad to see so few bakeries left, but a tribute to Esther and Joe that Barron's has survived and prospered.

Willie Murphy While not a staff member, I was a rep. first for Ranks and later up to July 2010 for Andrews Milling so I was selling to Barron's for forty years. It was always a pleasure to call there. Joe Barron knew his flour and demanded high standards, which of course we delivered. I remember he had a big pair of hands from kneading, with strong wrists which were useful to him when he rowed for Cappoquin. Mrs Barron would always make tea and you really couldn't leave without having some.

67

Staff members past and present

L-R: Margo Murphy, Joe Prendergast, Esther Barron, Eileen O'Donoghue. Milo Murray, Kevin Wilkinson, Marcia Power, Alan O'Donoghue, Lukasz Szewe, Anne Forbes, Marcus O'Halloran, Zbignien Rybinski, Susan Simpson, Victoria Barrett, Pat Grant, Mary Glavin, Bernie Organ, Dermot Dee, Anna Fraher, Bernadette Glavin, Breda Walsh, Miriam Cunningham, Helen Cunningham, John O'Rourke, Mary Casey, Ann Prendergast, Denis Murray, Sheena Wilkinson, Val Gates, Claire Walsh, Siobhan McCarthy, Gearóid Byrne, Paddy Murray, Emma Condon. Missing from photograph: Ramel Quilico, Caroline Ind.

Eily Ryan I worked in the old shop for over three years until 1980 when the bakery was in full swing. Joe Barron was baking then with Paddy Murray who started early in the morning so the bread came straight out of the ovens into the shop. They brought their delicious, warm aromas with them. I remember helping Esther to make Christmas cakes so I was always learning. I picked up a lot of tips. It was a nice place to work. We had groceries too such as sugar, butter and we got milk in so customers could get all they needed together. Esther used to drive the van at that time, delivering bread and groceries like her father before her. It was a Passat estate and we bought it later from her.

The customers were lovely, they came in every few days, some of them even every day, and we always knew what they would want. Some had a permanent order so they would get the crusty, even black, pans they wanted. However, there were times when we ran out. You couldn't always anticipate the volume of Battenbergs, fresh cream sponges, coffee cakes – all made by Esther herself. She even made my wedding cake. I really enjoyed the craic of talking to the customers. They would share a joke or some funny incident – always light and fun. It was the one job I really did love. Mrs Barron was a dote and I always got on well with Esther. They are all happy memories. I felt part of the family and was treated very well. I could go into their kitchen and make tea any time and Mrs Barron would always give me my dinner. She fed all of us working there. I still love the grinders. These loaves were always my favourites.

Bernadette Glavin (O'Rourke) I worked in the coffee shop for about twelve years until 1997. I remember being very busy, especially when the Melleray grotto was established. People came from all over the country for six weeks in the summer to pray at it. Having got spiritual sustenance they called to us in the coffee shop for more physical sustenance, enjoying Esther's innovation of serving soups and toasted sandwiches. I remember the doctors and nurses meeting in the coffee shop, as well as teachers and the workers at Cappoquin chicken factory. It was always busy. The smell of fresh bread was always there. I enjoyed the banter with customers. Many of them, like me, wanted to chat. There was great craic with the staff; the bakers were always great fun – Paddy 'Baker' Murray, John Power, Dermot Dee; and Joan Cahillane, Marcia Power(O'Donoghue) and Breda Walsh were the confectioners. We were always busy, but we found time for fun too. Esther was always coming up with ideas so we tried loads of new cakes and various ideas in the café. I made great friends there and most of us are still in touch.

Rody McGrath My father Willie was a well-known driver of the delivery van for Barron's. I took the odd Monday off school when he did deliveries. We went all the way up the Nire valley, close to Clonmel and would come back down, delivering to houses. Sometimes it would be just a dozen loaves, some butter and biscuits for a pretty long journey, but I suppose petrol was cheap.

Connie McGrath During school term I worked in the bakery, greasing pans for bread, and while Joe Barron delivered bread, I took the bracks out of the oven. I remember Michael McGrath, known as Sailor McGrath who was in the airforce, helping out one evening in the bakery. He stoked the oven as if it were a ship's, the oven overheated and all the bread was burned. I also remember one customer coming into the bakery and buying bread. Finding he was a few pence short, he was given credit, but returned later having weighed the bread and claimed it was light a few ounces and he didn't owe the money after all. Joe's sister Hess had no choice but to take his word for it. I would be sent to the shop on Hess' instructions to buy two thinly sliced pieces of ham for Joe Barron's supper. He would have this in a sandwich with a small bottle of stout after his day's work, and before the early morning start.

John O'Rourke I was in my late twenties when I started working as a driver in the 1980s. I'd load up and get to the shops which were opening at 8am and I'd have to come back to refill and by then the bracks and cakes would be ready. All the customers would be served by 12.30. I enjoyed it. You just wanted your wages at that age. The staff were good and Mrs Barron would be there and you'd see her, but she never interfered. We knew all our customers and whatever they asked for, we got it. Health bread was coming along at that time and because all the bread was so good, I knew it would last. I still buy it myself. A friend living in San Francisco brings over an empty suitcase and fills it with brown sodas and turnovers to take home with him. The bakery has been good for the town and Esther is good to the people. I had worked in the monastery before that delivering eggs, then there was the bread. Now I work in a bar delivering drink!

Helen Cunningham I worked in the house with Mrs Barron and also served in the coffee shop on Sundays and bank holidays. That was for ten years from 1978 and I enjoyed every hour of it. I was part of the community and that was a nice feeling. I enjoyed meeting customers and noticed how tourists came back each year. They loved the home baking. 'I hope you have plenty of those lovely scones,' they'd say, 'I'm back for them.' The minute I saw them, I'd recognise them and they me. It was a good stop for them on their way to Melleray or Killarney and they loved the sandwiches made from a nice pan. It was easy to make a good sandwich with it. I'm here for forty-two years and was great friends with Mrs Barron. I used to do the hoovering on Mondays and Fridays and she was always good to me when my six children were growing up.

Karen Kiely I worked in the coffee shop fifteen years ago for two years and the clearest memory I have is of Mrs Barron. She was getting a little frail at that stage and I would bring her dinner to her. She appreciated anything I did for her. A real lady.

Michael Fraher I grew up in Cappoquin and worked in the bakery after school doing odd jobs, sweeping up and loading vans. It was no big deal and I was glad of a few shillings. The Barrons were lovely to work for. Hessie was the darling of the house and looked after the shop, and let everyone know she was the boss! Every town in those days had a bakery and we say we have progress! People have lost a lot when you think about bakeries in other towns. The living was better then, less demanding. We had less, but we needed less. If we could keep everything close to home, it would be better for everyone. The difference in texture of good bread and poor is like chalk and cheese. It's all machines in the multiples these days.

71

Pat-a-cake, pat-a-cake, baker's man,

Bake me a cake as fast as you can;

Pat it and prick it, and mark it with B,

Put it in the oven for baby and me.

Bernie Organ I worked in the shop thirteen years ago for three or four years, part-time in the mornings which suited me when I had children. I was busy all the time and I loved my time there. The customers were great. One man from Cappagh used to come every day for his dinner and the district nurse came every day too. We had about eight daily regulars. At the time I was there I was on a diet, and in the mornings it was too early to eat anything sweet, so I couldn't indulge in everything I saw, but I always brought home the bread.

Breda Walsh I worked as a confectioner from 1989 to 1993 making doughnuts, scones, brown bread and fresh cream cakes which had to be filled by 9am. On Mondays we made Madeiras; we'd fill them on Tuesday. I loved making the cheesecakes and still do with strawberries liquidised with Philadelphia cheese. I could make them every day, they're so light, and I could eat a few slices too! Everything was and is made fresh, no preservatives, and you can taste the difference. The packet ones are terrible. The secret of good confectionery is creaming the butter or margarine and sugar for a long time. Butter keeps better in wedding cakes and I always use self-raising flour. I often made a football or soccer pitch cake. There was lots of work in them. I'm still asked to make wedding cakes. Joan Cahillane and I would be flat out all the time and Marcia Power came later and it really was a busy time there. Esther would have to help us out. When my sister married in 1992 Esther and I made the wedding cake. It was the hardest work I ever did, but you'd love it. The washing-up was the worst and you'd have to keep on top of it. You'd use loads of bowls. I always enjoyed the work and people like

Dermot Dee, John Power and Bernadette O'Rourke were always in good form. I would help out later in the coffee shop if it was busy. We all mucked in. We were a hard grafting lot. We made great friendships.

Alan O'Donoghue Working with the delivery van from 1994 to 2000 was one of the nicest jobs I had. The fresh smell of bread out of the oven at 4.30am was good compensation for the early start. At that time on a Saturday morning you'd see people coming back from nightclubs and they'd ask for bread for soakage after drinking. I lived across the road from the bakery so had two minutes to walk to work. Still, I was glad to have a nice, warm bakery to go to. I had good time for the customers. They were mostly supermarkets and shops, but I also enjoyed calling to the nuns at Glencairn. They were very private and would slide a shutter aside and then a two-tier shelved structure would appear and I would put their bread on it. At Christmas a nun would put a £10 note on it for me as it rotated back and I always had a chat with her. One of those special encounters.

Anthony Prendergast In the 1980s I worked for five years as a van driver for Barron's and would head off at 9am for Ballinamult Creamery, Knockmeal Co-op and Cappagh Co-op. I liked driving the van with its smell of the best bread in Ireland. It was good to deliver nice products. For some houses I'd leave bread on top of the pier, other houses would be taking six loaves for their big families. You'd have an idea of what they'd want and they'd leave a note for extras. I rarely had bread coming back in the van; it was lovely bread. It was a grand occupation. I couldn't say a word against the job or the people I worked for.

74

Alice Connery O'Donoghue From 1978 to 1980, I trained as a confectioner with Esther and eventually she let me off to do all the mixes on my own. I used to make the butterfly cakes – they were my favourite– and the almond and the custard slices too. I loved laying them out on trays for the shop. I also had the job of slicing the bread and wrapping it. Paddy 'Baker' Murray would be ahead of me in the mornings and there would be bread ready for slicing and wrapping. I had a thing inside me to do the wrapping as quickly as possible. It was like a race against myself to see how many loaves I could manage in an hour. I had to leave when I got married as I moved away from Cappoquin and didn't have a car. Given the choice I'd still be there, I loved it so much.

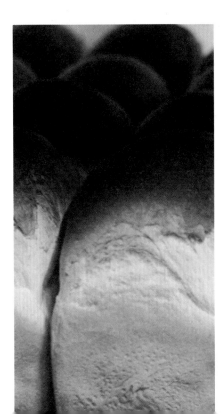

The Heartbeat of the Town **Customers Remember the Bakery**

Margaret Cahill

I played with Deirdre and Esther around the bakery before it started up at night. I was fascinated by the ovens, the huge spaces; the bricks of the ovens were like a big secret. We played Blind Man's Buff, there were great hiding places there, no such thing as safety regulations then! We felt free to run around, and didn't ever feel we were doing anything wrong. It felt magical, perhaps more dramatic as it was quite dark. The slicer intrigued me as there were two sides to it like bookmarks. Then the wrapping would be heated to make it stick. One time Esther and I thought it would be a good idea to make a face mask from yeast. We mixed it with water and put it on thickly over our faces. It started to get stiff and we had to give in and wash it off after a few minutes. I'm related to the Barrons as my grandmother on my mother's side was Hanora Collender and I always felt welcome in the bakery. Joe was always in a white coat and was bald, while Hess, who was very much in control, would be dressed in a white coat to her knees and had grey hair. There were lollipops, bonbons, bullseyes in jars which would be dispensed into small paper bags, and bread on the counter top and shelves at the back with apples squares, Chester cakes. I loved the hot cross buns.

There would be chocolate truffles the size of your fist at Christmas. We always bought their bread, two big lumps joined together with a lovely crust and sometimes a bubble of crust on the side. A sliced pan was a foreign object to us. We preferred to cut ours. Customers would arrive into the shop in turned down wellingtons, other women in smart herringbone costumes in town for the day. You'd rarely meet a stranger in those days.

Peggy Coffey

I'm fifty years a customer of the bakery, and I remember Joe Barron arriving at my home in the hinterland of Cappoquin. Joe would dispense buns in which I revelled and I looked forward to his banter. He was always in good form, it seemed. In my family of four, a lot of bread was consumed and we looked forward to other treats at the end of the week, something sweeter. These days I look forward to having my cup of coffee every Friday in the bakery café and stocking up on the buttermilk brown loaf.

Anna Fraher

The bakery was part of life in Cappoquin. The smell of fresh bread was mouthwatering and the shop always had lovely boiled sweets. I remember the staff wearing white coats and all the girls were nice, good fun, but always very polite.

Mary Phelan Ryan

I left Cappoquin at the age of ten or eleven, I'm now in my sixties, but one of my earliest memories is of the smell of bread baking in the village. I lived at the top of the main street and the aromas would drift up the street to meet us in the morning. It was a meeting place for us kids who were sent to buy the bread and I loved seeing all the bread and iced cakes laid out in rows. If we were out very late, we would look in through the open door of the bakery and see the fresh bread there, cooling. The odd time we would take a loaf and eat it on the way home. Of course we paid for it the next day. We were all honourable in those days and many doors were often open. As children it was all part of our lives. In the 1960s there were lovely iced buns and little tarts which were unusual to find in bakeries at the time, but mostly all we could afford was a good loaf of bread and I remember liking it a lot.

Fr Columban

I'm based in Mount Melleray and have been a fan of Barron's bread for the last ten years, since the baking of bread stopped in the monastery. There was a time when we were fully self-sufficient, but dwindling vocations means fewer people to do the work. The aim of the monks to be self-sufficient encouraged excellence in doing things for themselves. Esther uses techniques which are better than the new inventions. Her father Joe always struck me as a significant member of the community. He was devoted to his family and work, and with his good civic spirit, pulled his weight in the community. He and his wife brought up a lovely family whom we often met at mass here in Mount Melleray. They are our closest neighbours and we are glad to have their bread.

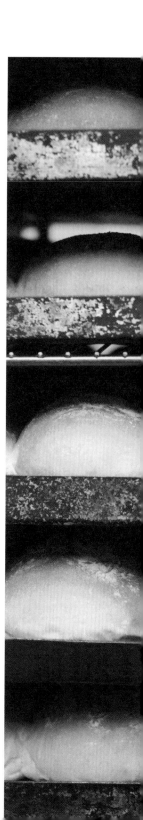

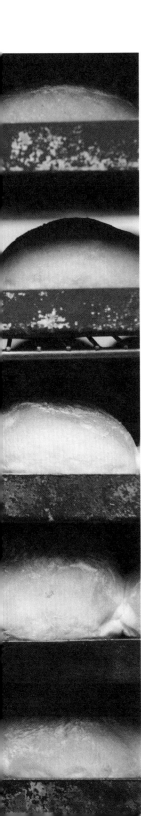

Brendan Kiely

As a friend of the family and a neighbour, I was always in and out of the bakery and between the ages of twelve and fourteen I would help Willie McGrath on deliveries. I never considered baking as a profession as the heat was too much for me. One tip I have for anyone delivering bread is to make sure to keep the windows of the van open. The heat of the bread makes it a hothouse. I remember in winter people bringing in their sheets to be dried by the heat in the bakery once the early morning's work was done – another social service provided by the family.

I was fascinated with the tins that had Barron's name embossed so the name came out on the side of the pans. For a while we made bread from Hovis flour which was malted and I loved it. I was fascinated by the way the dough had to be stretched for turnovers. I also remember the wonderful sight of the pans tossed out and left to cool before being sliced. Every batch seemed different. If anyone tried to put them through the slicer before they were cool, the slicer would tear them up and there was a terrible mess and waste. It was an efficient system as one person would be at each end of the slicer for counterweights, then the sliced bread would go into the wax wrapper. The wrapped bread would then go onto a heated plate which would melt some of the wax and seal it.

What I remember most was how particular customers were about what they wanted. They knew the difference between a tiled turnover and a tinned loaf – you couldn't palm anything off on them. Mr Barron was amazing to see working. One night in winter the electricity was cut off and of course the bakery couldn't operate. Mr Barron went back to basics and got briquettes and coal and lit them around the inside of the oven and cooked the bread in two batches. It was a super-human effort. The bread that came out was quite different to the usual, a throw-back to the old days. Mr Barron was also really interested in sport and was a good rower himself. I remember him giving time off to Paddy Murray, the baker, who was a great rower.

Thomas McCarthy

I grew up as a customer of Barron's but as I delivered newspapers and milk around Cappoquin at the age of nine and ten, I was also a witness to early morning activities. In its earliest stirring the town heard the clunking of the door of the *Cork Examiner* van and Barron's bread van opening and closing, the bread being loaded in and taken out. It was the beating heart of the town; the first heartbeat bringing life to the town. We were the morning creatures, along with the badgers. In those days Cappoquin was a thriving

79

town, tearing busy, in fact the busiest in west Waterford. One hundred and twenty people were employed in the bacon factory and there were two secondary schools. P.C. Cahill was a master tailor who had worked on Saville Row in London and made hunting jackets and bespoke sports jackets.

There was also a saddlery which certainly was not part of my life; I was a townie, I never managed to get in the door. My family came from the poorest part of town – Twin Bog. My family had been brought from the Béara peninsula in 1704 to work on a farm. Many Béara McCarthy families were transported into the Déise. There were also the Lonergan Brothers on Upper Main Street where people would congregate to chat. There would even be a queue, as some people wouldn't go in while others were there to hear their business. When I did the first reading of my first book in UCC in 1978, I referred to Cappoquin as a small village. I was reminded by a member of the audience that Cappoquin was never a village, but a town. Of course Steamers' Quay in Cappoquin was a place steamers came to from Youghal to dock at since 1878. There was quite a river industry. Cúl an Smután, now called Smutawn on Melleray Road, was where the burning embers of the oak woods were used as charcoal for industry. Pierce's Plough Foundry of Wexford started in Cappoquin. Cappoquin is in some of my poetry, and

in Joyce's *Ulysees* we find a few mentions of Cappoquin in part of the famous soliloquy. Michael Cavanagh, the Fenian poet and composer, wrote about the river. His statue is located across the street from Barron's Bakery. Pádraig Denn the nineteenth century Irish scholar is buried in the graveyard of St Mary's Catholic Church and of course Molly Keane spent time in Cappoquin. It was Sir John Keane who defended *The Tailor and Ansty*.

My cousin John and my favourite treat every Thursday in the late 1950s and early 1960s was to buy the *Hotspur, Beano* and *Victor*. I was earning enough from my deliveries for the Fraher sisters' newsagents for the comics and some of Barron's Chester cake, and we'd go to my grandmother's house to eat it. It seemed to have an irreducible amount of delight: we seemed to be able to cut and cut it, and there always seemed to be more from it. I adored Barron's shop, then an exotic emporium of smells. Until I found out recently in New York, I didn't realise that one of those scents was cinnamon. I would go there with my mother and Aunt Maggie, all of us townies. Joan Barron was a beautiful, elegant person, genteel, old-fashioned; all the family was considered fine and refined. The quality of the bread has always been fabulous, quite different to others – weightier, with more purchase in the texture. I lived for a while with my grandmother who was blind and she had

a huge open fire where a pot of potatoes could hang on a steel arm, and we would toast Barron's bread on a long prong, like a garden fork. I married a Cork woman so I have no hope of returning to live there, but Cappoquin is a place in my imagination.

Kevin McCarthy

Cappoquin has always had a fantastic tradition of hard work and industry. Barron's Bakery is a survivor from the days when the town was a hive of locally owned businesses, including a saddlery, two tailors, a barber, cobbler, several blacksmiths, coopers and drapers. Industrially, there has hardly been a town so small anywhere else in Ireland that has had so many successful industries. These have ranged from iron smelting and cannon manufacture in the early 1600s to wheel and carriage making, farm machinery production, bacon curing (twice), poultry processing, plastic moulding, precision engineering and more. In some cases, the buildings are there as a reminder of the great tradition of enterprise in the town, not least in the three-storey buildings and traditional shopfronts which still adorn some of Main Street.

From the 1940s, the war and short-sighted economic protectionism, compounded by new regulations after we joined the EEC in the 1970s, created various challenges for our industries. The closure of the railway in 1967 and rise of car ownership and of shopping centres in nearby large towns also put some nails in the coffin of Cappoquin's commercial life.

From 2000, new challenges like the loss of the town's secondary school and the decision by both major banks to leave the town as part of a rationalisation process did serious damage, and that was when times were good for the national economy. With the current recession, pub life, and indeed the future of many business and services we have taken for granted, are now under threat. There is a great sense of community bonding in Cappoquin, and great support for a huge range of local activities, groups and clubs. People here realise that we must do things for ourselves as much as we can, that this place and its people are worth fighting for, whatever others or other bodies might think. Hopefully, this kind of spirit, including ongoing support for our local shops, will see Cappoquin re-emerge as a viable economic and social entity out of this recession, and we will all be able to bask in the sunlight outside Barron's, sipping our coffees and telling our grandchildren all about the IMF, bailouts and the like. In days of great uncertainty, we need some certainties to cling to, and Barron's bread needs to be one of those for a long time to come.

81

Monsignor Michael Olden

I was born in Cappoquin and grew up in the 1930s on Main Street. I recall going to school aged four or five and getting the smells of the baking in the town. At work early, the bakeries provided a comforting aroma on the sleepy streets. I remember being sent on messages to the shop and how immaculately clean Barron's was (unfortunately this was remarkable for the time). Hess would always be dressed in a long, white coat and maybe a white cap or hat, so obviously clean. She was chatty, more so than others to small children. She asked questions and seemed interested in me, which I liked. I was always happy to go there. Joe was a hardworking man, not big on socialising, but he was friendly. He had a lovely voice. My uncle Jimmy Olden, who was friendly with Joe, had a sweet tooth and his favourite was Barron's Chester cake. He would send me for it as he said it was the best Chester cake in Munster. He didn't travel far to make comparisons, but he told everyone who came near him how good it was and how it was like a meal for his tea – and not too sweet. During the war flour quality was terrible and dirty looking. Somehow, every weekend, Joe Barron managed to have an amount, albeit limited, of white flour and some of us were privileged to get bread made from it. To this day I remember that weekend loaf – like heaven to me, and a marvellous treat. My mother would ration it and we had it for Sunday breakfast. Joe

Barron went to great effort to make the best of what they could get and share it around. I recall going next door for a chat with the saddler, and I'm delighted that as a café it's a talking shop again. Cappoquin, we always boasted, had the best bread in Ireland. The town wouldn't have been the same without it. It's a great tribute to the Barrons that they were part of that richness and that they have survived and prospered. As a boy, I would go to the railway station every day at 4pm to see the train arrive. If I behaved myself I was allowed into the signal box with a man called Kelleher. From there I could see everything. We had no television in those days and we would watch people saying their goodbyes to those leaving on their way to Waterford maybe to catch a boat to England. We saw the supplies for Barron's arriving and errand boys arriving to collect yeast for the bread. Each generation has modernised the bakery a little and taken it a step further in mechanisation without losing the core artisan feel. It is fortunate that Esther married Joe Prendergast as they have both grown in knowledge about the business.

83

Sr de Lourdes

My longest memory is of getting Barron's bread from them, at first delivered to us, then later, as our community diminished, collecting it ourselves from the bakery. Joe was one of the grandest men in Cappoquin, top of the bunch, a lovely, gentle, gracious man. He would never offend anybody. And a lovely singer. He was generous and I'm sure there were many poor people up in the area near Mount Melleray who benefitted from that generosity. He was loved by everybody in the town.

Kieran O'Connor

I lived across the road from Barron's and was the youngest in my family, as Esther was. We should have made a match! When I'd come home from a night out I'd hear the noise of the bakery and Pat the Baker might be going to work. I remember the smell of the bread going to school. I was overawed by the bakery – it seemed huge and the scale of what they produced was quite amazing to me. I watched the peel moving the bread into the oven like a huge oar.

In some ways it saddens me that we took it all for granted and that we don't still have the two tailors, Thomas and Noel Lonergan, who sat cross-legged in the window, Geoff Gambon the shoemaker, Keating's saddlery and John Rea the blacksmith.

Aunty Hessie was quite a character, I was afraid of her when I was younger. Joe often came to our house to watch television or listen to the matches on the radio with my father. He was a huge Waterford hurling fan. I remember the 1963 Waterford v Kilkenny final. I remember the train arriving at 4pm on its way to Rosslare and people crying and saying goodbye to those leaving for England.

Deirdre Quirke (O'Connor)

I was born across the road from Barron's and was the only girl amongst four boys so I was glad of the company of the Barron sisters, especially Deirdre who was my age. I was known as Deirdre Googoo as we had a chicken factory. We often slept in each other's houses. I remember Mrs Barron (Joan) as a real lady who was always respectful to everyone. Even though she was involved in the business she seemed to have time to read us stories. Aunt Hessie was different; she seemed to be the gate-keeper of the business and wasn't so easy-going. When she wasn't looking we'd rob a queen cake. I loved the hot crusty bread and wouldn't like it a day old as some did. Aunt Hessie would say, 'It's not old, it's cold!' I remember the window beautifully decorated with cakes and candles. In the 1960s the rosary was often said in the Barron household and if I were there at 7pm any day I would have to join in. However, as we didn't say it at home, I'd get it wrong, but no-one made me feel bad.

Deirdre was responsible for me getting into the social whirl and ended up being my bridesmaid. She would come with me to our rented house in Tramore during holidays from boarding school and they would bring me on picnics with them. My mother and Mrs Barron went on holiday together to what we thought of as exotic places such as Jersey. As they got older they were both in the Widows' Association. What I noticed about the Barrons was their work ethic. 'To work is to pray' seemed to be the motto there. The girls seemed to work long hours and drove the car to deliver as hardly anyone else had cars in those days. Mrs Barron was a progressive thinker and I reckon she kept a lot of stories of the girls' antics from her husband. I would watch rugby matches with Mr Barron in front of the fire. Coming from a family of boys, I was into sport and his daughters weren't. There were always cats and kittens in the Barron household and one day Esther and I put one of them into the oven to dry its fur. We were innocent then.

Ann Quann Donovan

As a child I was in and out of Barron's a lot, playing with Deirdre, in their huge kitchen with red tiles on the floor. We were never allowed into the bakery. It was a place of mystery for me and I always wondered what was happening there. I remember Hessie Ha'Penny being strict,

yet I loved going in to her to buy bread, and to experience the great smell in the shop. Once when I came home from England I bought an ordinary sliced pan and my father thought it really terrible that I bought anything but Barron's bread. Quality pays off. I think Esther has proven her point, and now one of my daughters won't eat anything else.

Marie Murphy

I remember Joe Barron arriving on Mondays to deliver bread. There were eleven of us in the family and we'd be hanging off my mother's skirt. I think he felt sorry for my mother and would give us all Peggy's Legs to keep us quiet.

85

John Arrigan

In the 1940s I would be sent to Barron's by my mother and grandmother to buy bread. It was delicious and golden, with a particular taste like no other. I could never resist breaking off some of the crust on the way home and would get into trouble for doing it. I'm reminded of how de Valera used to have the same problem, as did a friend of his who often went with him to a bakery for loaves of bread. Dev's solution was to eat his piece off the loaf and then give the loaf to his friend. His friend would do the same. Then, when he got home he told his mother that another fella ate it. I loved the sign on the side of Barron's van which said, 'Half a loaf is better than no bread and there is no bread better than Barron's'. There were no marketing consultants in those days, but Joe Barron knew his business. They say that in France Saint Honora is the patron saint of bread. I'd say Esther Barron is Ireland's.

Deirdre Arrigan

It was only in the last few years that I realised that brack was not always Barron's. When I was given barm brack I thought it was called Barron Brack. We ate nothing else, and it's still my favourite even though I don't live in Cappoquin anymore. My father brings home plenty for all of us when he visits his home town.

Margaret Quann Foley

For me Barron's was a magical place. It looked massive though I'm sure it wasn't, but to me as a child that's how it seemed. Their Chester cake was synonymous with Cappoquin. I remember a bell like a bicycle bell would ring when we went in the door and I always thought they were very trusting as we would often be left alone in the shop to wait for Hessie to come out and serve us. We could be standing there for five minutes looking in awe at the rectangular tall jars of sweets with their screwcaps. We all thought Joe was super-human as he worked all night, but still managed to find time to play with the Brass and Reed Band and to sing in the choir. I remember him delivering in the van too, not just bread, but the weekly *Dungarvan Leader* newspaper. I looked forward to the lovely display of iced Christmas cakes in the window at Barron's and I have enjoyed the benefits of Esther giving Christmas cakes for many raffles for charity. The family was always generous. Today I always eat Barron's bread because it's so much more pure and wholesome than other sliced pans which always have to be toasted to give them flavour. One slice of Barron's is very satisfying.

Michael O'Connor

I was born across the road from the bakery and my Monday job as a seventeen-year-old was to bring a cart on wheels to collect eggs from the bakery. They would have been collected on Joe's bread round, having been bartered with for bread and other supplies. I had to fill the 30-egg cartons, there would be dozens of them each day and I would have to negotiate with Joe's sister Hessie about price.

Rose Sargent

I'm a customer for fifty years now. One Christmas day in Cappoquin there was no electricity and we had a raw turkey to deal with. Barron's obliged us with the huge oven and my husband went and collected the cooked one and spilled the fat all over the place. That wasn't our best Christmas but we were glad to have a cooked turkey. We had lived in the station house for twenty years and sold it to Joe and Esther. I remember the signal cabin and a dry storehouse on the side rail where the tea, coffee and sugar would be stored until it was collected. These days I enjoy meeting pals after mass for coffee in Barron's café, along with some sweet treat I allow myself. It's a great asset to Cappoquin.

Mary Nicholson

I remember my late husband preferring the black, crusted loaf. I've lived for forty-four years in the town and Barron's is a real landmark.

Maura Keating

We were neighbours and customers all our lives, and my parents before me. I knew Joe and Joan as nice, gentle people and I always considered Barron's bread the best. And there was Aunt Hessie who always wore a white coat. I saw a repeat of a television programme with Barron's featured with the chef Richard Corrigan. That gave us all a thrill to see it looking so well and appreciated by him.

Canon Nugent

I'm a customer for twenty years and have known the family socially as well, especially as we were all interested in heritage. I joke a lot with Esther. She's vivacious and colourful and her husband Joe is a gentleman, very kind. I always experienced the utmost courtesy from the family who were interested in people, with full focus on the customer. The ovens do a special job and I only buy Barron's bread, never the sealed loaves produced commercially. I enjoy a cup of coffee too and when I was more mobile often went for lunch while on my rounds, not just for the bread, but for the confectionery. The quality of their Christmas pudding was special and I officiated at lots of weddings which had the wedding cakes supplied by Barron's. I found their Christmas cakes ideal as gifts during the festive season. But my favourite of all is the apple strudel which is well up to Austrian standards which I experienced many times. It brings me back to green summer fields around Kitzbul and, halfway up the mountains, the sounds of the cows' bells, a church, a café and apple strudel.

There is something wondrous
in the taste of bread.

It is so ordinary yet it is so good.
It is very democratic.
It nourishes the poor and the rich.
It goes well with meat or fish, with fruit or cheese.
It may return three times a day to the table;
it may even stay there all day long.

Yet it never outstays its welcome.

LADISLAS ORSY

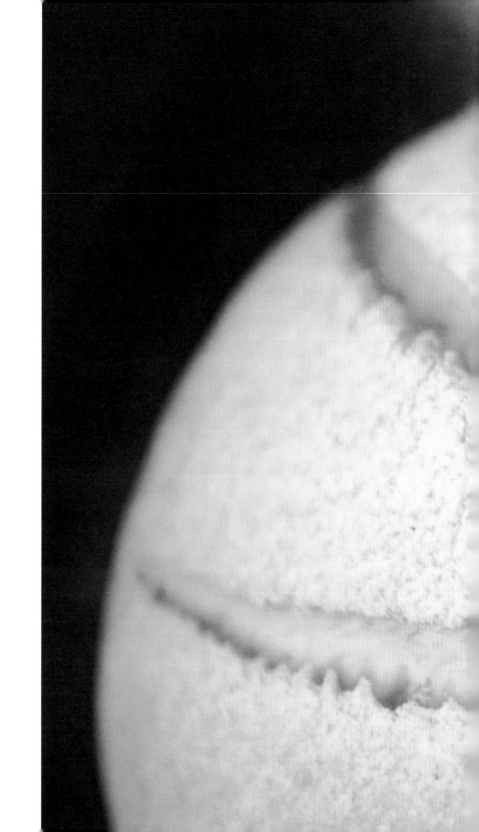

Bridget Looby

I'm eighty-seven now and have been eating Barron's bread since I've been able to eat! I live five miles from any town and Joe Barron delivered every Tuesday and Saturday. We looked forward to his visits in the van and we would all have a slice of bread as soon as it arrived. As there were no cars at the time we were glad of the butter, tea, sugar, jam and the newspaper which would be delivered too. In those days it was unusual to look out the window and see a car. It was only the priest and doctor who would have one. We used pony and traps or we often walked four miles to the town.

Eddie Fraher

As a young lad doing the shopping for my mother the wonderful array of cakes, tarts, loaves and pans were eye-catching. Of course the big glass jars of boiled sweets also caught the eye of a young lad. Another striking feature was the spotlessly clean white coats on the ladies serving in the shop. Barron's Bakery was certainly a landmark in the business life of Cappoquin in my youth as it is today, all credit to them.

Jenny Fraher

I was terribly fond of Hess, Joe and Joan. Deirdre was a tearaway and, as we lived around the corner from the bakery, the two of us got up to mischief. A big tray of bracks still warm from the oven would be brought along the street, door to door to customers. They had lovely cherries. I can see them now, still hot. I remember that turkeys were cooked by Barron's for the old folk's party.

Mary Coughlan

We have a deli and sell Barron's bread every day. The Barron girls were around my age so I saw the development of the bakery including the conversion of the saddlery. I remember the old shop and going through it into the back to the house. It was a busy household and everyone worked very hard. I remember Margo as the confectioner. They made my wedding cake. It was in a horseshoe shape thirty-nine years ago and I know they had to get the tins especially from Hurley's in Youghal. I remember that on Sundays there would be queues out the gate for Dr Winnie White and for Barron's Bakery. Dr Winnie was a marvellous person who people called on for the slightest ailment, even on Sundays. Barron's also opened on Sundays and we would leave in our list of groceries while we went to mass. Margo, Siobhan and I would get dressed up for the dance in The Boathouse, the girls rushing their work so they could get out. One night we borrowed one of the vans to get us to a dance. Somewhere between Midleton and Tallow one of the wheels passed us out and we had to come home. We had some fun.

Biddy Tobin

I came to Melleray from Cappoquin when I was two and a half and, as I'm eighty-eight now, I have seen a few changes in the town. Our bread was delivered by Joe Barron and his uncle before him, on Tuesdays and Saturdays. There were goodies as well as bread, and the buns those days were quite a treat. There were big changes in the war years. No petrol was the obvious one and Joe delivered with a pony and a sort of a van pulled behind it. When he'd reach us in winter in dark nights he would have a lantern on the side of the van. We used to watch for the van on the boreen. There was no tarmacadam then and we would watch him approaching slowly from the distance. Only the priest and the doctor would have cars in those days and we had no electricity or running water. I don't know how we managed as there was a sugar and flour shortage too, no white flour in fact. We were lucky we had our own veg, milk and eggs and we made our own butter. On the farm we worked long hours for little return and everyone was the same. Gradually comforts came but we hardly noticed them. It's amazing what man is capable of. Nowadays perhaps we even take good bread for granted.

Mary Glavin

I live in Lismore and was originally from Ballysaggart. I grew up with Barron's bread as even though our house was too isolated for our own delivery, it was left at a neighbour's house for us. Frank Crotty was the van driver, I remember. The highlight was him coming with the fresh bread. We'd be sent to collect the few pan loaves from the neighbour and we'd nearly have one eaten by the time we got home, picking at it. My late mother sold eggs to Joan Barron and I had the job of washing them first and wrapping each one in a sheet of the *Cork Examiner* which we would cut into squares. We'd sit around the table wrapping them and would get a clatter around the ear if we broke one. After working in Faber-Castell pencil factory in Fermoy, I was in the coffee shop for about six months and met lovely people such as Joan Cahillane, Bernie Glavin and Breda Walsh. Esther Barron was thorough; she knew her business. I'd wash the display cabinet and often I would have to shine it up just a bit more. She was a great teacher. Three evenings out of five a man would come into the coffee shop at 5.50 for a toasted special and would stay until 6.30. I couldn't show that I was dying to close up and wash the floor. When I have friends staying they always buy the bread and bracks to take home and I'm glad to see the Dungarvan stall buzzing with activity. People go for the homemade quality. It has more taste. Esther is such a personality. I don't know where she gets her energy. It makes a difference when you meet a smiling person when you are shopping.

Arthur K. Maderson

I spend my life as a painter between Le Vigan, a small town on the River Arre which commands a wooded valley in the High Cevenne, south of France, and Cappoquin, even smaller, which nestles on the lower slopes of the Knockmealdown Mountains on the glorious River Blackwater. One of the highlights of living in France is the ten minute walk to both the boulangerie (baker's shop) and the patisserie (cake shop). Of course it is unfair and ungentlemanly to compare mistresses, and in truth both have their own delightful charms, but Cappoquin tips the scale as Barron's Bakery has both an excellent boulangerie and patisserie combined. I lost my sense of smell perhaps five or six years ago and, as is inevitable, I harbour my nostalgic checklist of smells I miss, smells which curiously only return, often vividly, in dreams. Close to the top of this list is a very early walk into Cappoquin during the dog-end of summer, passing as if on automatic pilot Barron's Bakery with its sumptuous wafts of freshly baked bread and cakes drifting through the fine autumn mist. I had better stop for fear of tantalising myself further, but simply thank Esther and Joe for providing those memories, which still linger there.

91

Jimmy Collender

My family had the pub next door to the bakery (my mother Mary still lives there) and we always appreciated the sweets and buns which were always well displayed and Joe would often give us sweets and Esther gave us buns. We used to bottle our own porter and had a mini-shed beside the bakery. At that time there was a world of shops in Cappoquin.

Kathleen McGrath

Though I'm forty-three years in Cappoquin I'm still an 'import' and lived out of town in Affane. My aunt remembers deliveries by pony and trap and later the van. As my husband Denis was with CIE he was gone all day. That meant I was grounded and was very glad to see Mrs Barron or her daughters arrive in the van three times a week. It was a lovely service: you always got what you wanted and as Denis was a smoker they delivered his cigarettes too. When my son John started school we were standing outside once for at least an hour waiting for the school bus. Instead the bread van arrived driven by Deirdre Barron who reminded me there was no school on Our Lady of Mercy's feast day. We could have been waiting all day only for her. They always had the news of the day and we were glad to get it. It was often our only way of knowing if there was a bereavement in the area too. I used to have

to avoid Joe Barron when there were matches on. I'm from Kilkenny and Joe was from Tipperary.

Anna Crotty

When the railway station was still operating in Cappoquin a lot of my relatives would come to visit by train. As soon as they arrived they would be off to Mrs Barron to put in an order to take home. They loved the Tipsy and Chester cakes as well as the bread, and as a result lots of people in London knew all about Barron's, even though they had never been to Ireland. My uncle Terry is eighty-eight and recalls how Mrs Barron always remembered all our relatives. She'd have the farmers' butter and sweets for us, and we got a loaf of bread every day. We loved the blaas and the queen cakes too.

Helen Wall

I remember when tea and coffee were short during the war we would swap clothes for some with Loretto and Francis Bolger who had a big family. My late brother was in a wheelchair for quite a while and he would take my niece into Barron's every day to buy her whatever treat she wanted.

Sheila Foley

I remember the film *One of Ourselves* being filmed in the bakery and was able to get a sneaky look at it being done which was great for me. I loved getting good sandwiches from Barron's to bring to matches and my sister in England always had to have turnovers brought to her.

Ben Murphy

Locals owning and running a business is so much better than having multinational corporations. The bakery is a great asset to the town, it adds another dimension to it. I like the idea of old style bread, tried and tested, cooked traditionally and yet from a place that's run so professionally.

Tom O'Sullivan

The Barron daughters would come to our farm with their father or Willie McGrath who drove the van. The girls would often stay with us for about half an hour while the delivery was done to other farms nearby. My mother baked scones and they would have them with tea, especially on cold winter days. But none of them fell for me! We were all a bit too young at the time. My mother made butter and we were glad to be able to sell it to Barron's and to have it collected and the bread delivered. We only had a tractor at that time.

Mary Fives

The coffee shop is the best thing that ever happened to Cappoquin, for both passersby and locals. I only live up the road, but I go to Barron's for coffee. I met one woman recently whose four children are now going to school. When she dropped the last one off having been tied to them for so many years, she celebrated, saying, 'I'm off now to Barron's for a cup of coffee.' We were a baking family, living in the country; we made our own cakes, but we always bought their bread, 'real' bread which has never changed, whatever the recipe is.

Michael Ormonde

I lived in Salterbridge and worked for the Knockmeal creamery in Cappoquin from 1963 up to 1976. I had the Melleray run and would collect milk from about sixty small farmers and deliver Barron's bread at the same time as part of the creamery's service. There were regular orders, and then if people wanted anything different, they'd leave a note on the churn. I'd deliver fifty, sixty or seventy pans and never came home with any. Then later in the evening I used to return the empty milk churns and if anyone wanted more bread they would let me know. There were eighteen working there at the time, but that creamery went into liquidation and now even in Cappoquin creamery employment has reduced to two, but at least it's still there.

93

Mary McGrath

When I was nine or ten every Saturday I used to go in the grey van to help Willie McGrath with his deliveries. I loved it because we had no car at that time, so it was exciting for me. We delivered to another McGrath family and I remember how nice they were. Mrs Bridget McGrath would come down the path to meet us with her canvas bag and fill it with seven or eight pans, porridge and the newspaper. Little did I know that my future husband was one of the children who ate that bread. I met him later playing badminton. I remember working in the shop too, mainly getting messages for Mrs Barron and I recall Lolo Cahill coming in for her special small pan and Ann Mason who liked the crust so burnt it was like charcoal. We looked after everyone in those days and we had huge respect for them. That's how we were brought up.

Mossie Healy

Forty or fifty years ago Joe Barron in his white jacket and sometimes a tweed hat would arrive to us in Ballyhane twice a week and he would give us young lads a couple of buns. We looked forward to seeing the van as we only had bicycles. My mother and father would come out to meet him as they enjoyed the craic with him and the talk about sport. It was all great fun.

Margaret Troy

My dad worked in the bakery as he had done in Madden's in Lismore before my mother died. He was lucky to be able to work in Cappoquin. To have a local bakery in our town is something special and I remember the fourteen of us in the family enjoying the ring and the basket pans. These days I'm in the coffee shop every day meeting my pals for a brown scone and coffee.

Mary Foley

Every day of my married life I have called to Barron's for a pan. It's a third of my husband's diet and now we give it to our two grandsons who love it toasted with beans or for egg sandwiches. When I was younger I had to buy it for my mother and I remember Joe Barron as a jolly man and Joan as a lovely woman.

Johnny Prendergast

Yes, aged ninety-seven, I must be the oldest customer of Barron's. I've been eating it as long as I can remember. Other bread may be half the price, but it's not a quarter of its value. As a farmer and a contractor with eight employees I was a big customer as I liked to keep the men happy and well fed. They all got Barron's bread during the day. That's going back a long way, to a time when in 1925 you could buy a copy of the *Cork Examiner* for a penny. I lived near Affane, a mile outside Cappoquin, and I bought my first car in 1946 – a Ford Prefect – and I could go to Cappoquin to pick up the bread. I'm now living forty miles away near Tramore and I still have to get Barron's bread. There's no other like it.

Pat Conroy

I was a very good friend of Joan Barron's, and as she got older I would sit with her and hear all about the workings of the bakery. She would walk me through the bakery which she was very proud of, especially the brick ovens. She enjoyed the business and was ninety-three when she died. I'm eighty-nine now and I still miss her. She worked hard, but enjoyed every moment of it. My mother was the antiques buyer for Maceys in New York so I was brought up by my grandmother in Fermoy. She had a private maternity practice there. I've enjoyed my life to the full. I was married and had two children and now I have grandchildren and even five great grandchildren. These days I go to Barron's coffee shop for my daily cappuccino. I'm hooked on it!

95

The odds of going to the store for a loaf of bread

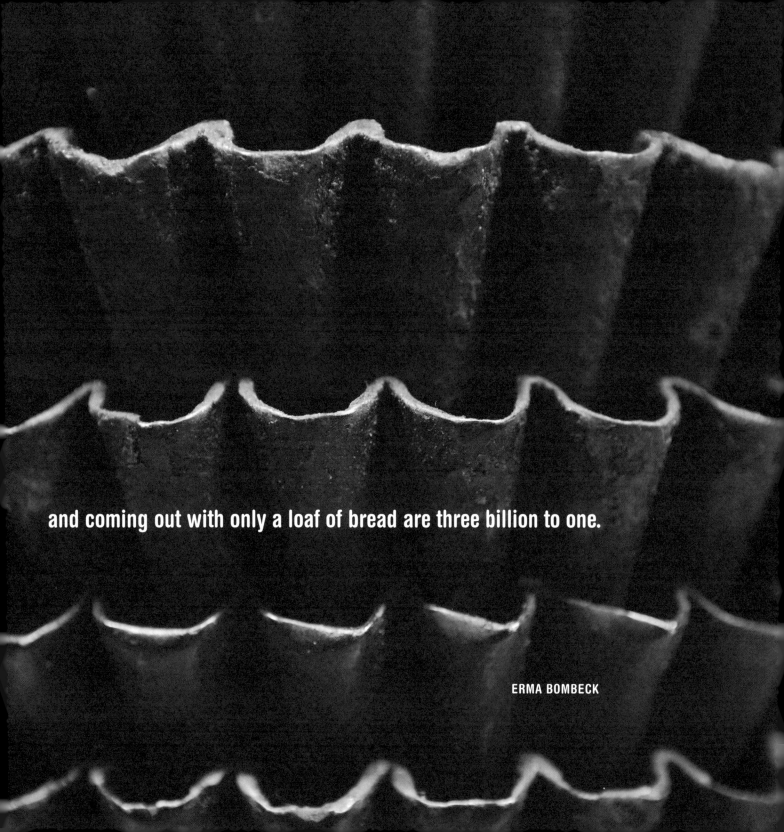

and coming out with only a loaf of bread are three billion to one.

ERMA BOMBECK

Kathleen Kearney

I was a district public health nurse and Joe Barron was one of my first patients. I looked forward to calling to both Joan and Joe Barron. It was a hardworking, hospitable household. There was always a lovely smell of coffee and baking. I retired in 2000 and when Esther started to do lunches I told everyone if they wanted to see me, they would find me there any day.

Maura O'Donnell

I had twelve children and lived in a small cottage in Ballygallane Upper, Lismore. I looked forward to the bread van coming. It was hard to get into town with twelve kids. If I was a bit short, Joe would never mind and he always had some boiled sweets for the kids. Bracks were our treat. Mrs Lehane in the town was generous too with loose biscuits. We had potatoes and turnips from nearby farms, and they would give us a gallon of milk. They were great helping times. Flour bags from the bakery were good for making sheets for cots. There was great wear in them. I always felt that God was with us in wicked bad times as we had no sickness. I always say the Angelus. I know there's a God there and that he is good. I have a fierce belief in holy water. We were always outside, making our own amusement. There was more freedom then. I never had to tell the kids to mind the cars. It's a long way from having no toilet to the mobile phones of today. Our kids loved the bread crusts.

Children throw them away now as if they are afraid of chewing. Now I have thirty-five grandchildren and six great grandchildren.

Mary O'Rourke

Times were hard in a cottage on the side of the road with a family of ten. When Joe Barron came in the van he'd give us bread and cigarettes even if we didn't have the money. He came in all kinds of weather, even when it was frosty. Willie McGrath drove the van after Joe and then Joan Barron, then Siobhan, then Esther. May God give Joe a good bed in Heaven. My son John drove the bread van and Bernadette worked in the coffee shop so we were quite involved throughout the years.

Molly McCarthy

I was born in 1928 and went to primary school in Cappoquin. Joe baked early as the creamery cars would come and he would need to have bread for them. It was lovely bread. We'd always bring some home with us on our way home from school and we'd have half a loaf eaten on the way home on the four-mile walk. We used to have the stations every few years which meant feeding twenty-five or thirty people for breakfast. We always had a huge brack from Barron's and plenty of their bread and of course their seed loaf. We had a butter loaf too in case someone didn't like the seeds. My wedding cake was made by Barron's in 1954.

Tommie McCarthy

I was a young lad of seventeen when my father built the brick ovens for Barron's and did the renovations to the house and stables to accommodate them. It was interesting work and it's good to see the ovens are still working well. Joe Barron married Joan when I was working on the house. My father was a builder like his father before him, but in the Hungry 1940s I couldn't serve my time fully as there was no work. I went to the north of England to work in the coalmines and became a fully fledged collier. I earned £22 a week when the average wage in Ireland was thirty shillings. We worked hard for it at the coalface and there were men there who were only forty or fifty and looked like old men, barely able to walk without running out of puff. I got an offer to become a mining engineer but it would have meant spending another five years in the mines and I thought it wasn't worth it. I joined the British army and am glad to be back living in Cappoquin now to enjoy what I can. I'm eighty-four and as long as I can throw my feet on the floor from the bed I know I'm lucky.

Billy Houlihan

In the 1950s I delivered milk every day to the creamery in Cappoquin. Part of the daily routine was a visit to Barron's bakery to purchase their delicious hand-baked bread.

When they started their delivery service, Tuesdays and Fridays were eagerly awaited when Siobhan Barron called to Lyre, Tour and Monamon, her van laden down with freshly baked bread. As the time approached for the arrival of the van one of the children would rush to collect the order: two white and a brown. I have the pleasure these days of introducing this wonderful product to our grandchildren. A fry cooked on the Aga on a Sunday morning served with lots of toasted Barron's brown and white bread is the firm favourite and the bakery is a wonderful part of our heritage. Long may it continue to flourish.

Margaret Casey

I lived in Melleray when the van would arrive with the goodies. My elderly mother sold eggs to Mr Barron and he would sell them on as he went along his journey. We would take delivery of bread for the Rawlins who lived down a boreen, so when I got old enough I delivered it to them in a white flour bag. My most vivid memory was the Saturday delivery of bread and sausages for dinner that evening. My late father wouldn't eat anything but Barron's bread and when he broke his hip I had to slice and butter their bread and bring it to him in the hospital in Ardkeen.

Molly and Tommie McCarthy with their Barron's wedding cake, 1954

Mary Hely

My grandparents established our pharmacy business in 1825 so the two families go back a long way. There was always one from each family in school together. Thirty or forty years ago I remember Daddy giving the brown bread to his racing greyhounds – you couldn't give white bread to them as it can cause epilepsy in that particularly sensitive breed. My two mongrel dogs will eat anything, but they prefer a fresh brown pan with butter and marmalade – like us.

Ina Hayes

As a young woman I worked across the street from the bakery and could see all the activity of the bakery. Siobhan would come over to us as she loved using our typewriter which was a novelty at the time. Things were relaxed in the days when I first came to Cappoquin at the age of ten. I remember the thrill of getting one of their barm bracks at Christmas time. I still love it, toasted with lots of butter. Another favourite was the gingerbread. These days I go to the coffee shop to meet my friends. It's wonderful to see it all still going strong. Joe Prendergast is a great worker and a huge asset to the business.

Tom Feerick

The Barrons have been smart and have moved with the times as businesspeople and with their development of different types of bread. I came to Cappoquin as a pharmacist in 1964 and I'd hold them in high esteem as one of the traders who have always been good to do business with. Not many have survived from the early days and it's good to see that Joe has such a flair for marketing to suit their current needs. Cappoquin had a pool of working people for a long time, from Pierce's Plough Foundry to the bacon factory. The Barrons have always been generous to the community centre.

Helena Jeffries

I blew in fifty years ago having lived on Cathedral Road in Cork. I was friends with Joan Barron and often went away with her on trips as part of the Widows' Association. She would come every Sunday to take me for a drive. The people of Cappoquin welcomed me when I arrived and Joan was a great friend. I miss her and my neighbours on Tivoli Terrace who have passed away. I'm eighty-two now and have never used any other bread. I go for coffee and a sit down in the coffee shop and always buy a brack which keeps me going for the week.

Phil Heffernan (Egan)

My earliest memory is of going to Barron's with my mother to get bread. It seemed like a small shop to me and I remember Hess behind the counter. I would pull bits off the loaf on the way home. Coming home from the pub at 1am I remember the smell of bread which would make me hungry. Barron's was always there. Joe was a household name. My son was delighted to see the coffee shop starting. He wanted to go there every day, it was such a novelty in Cappoquin. I remember Joe leading the Corpus Christi procession on a day so hot the tarmac melted into our sandals.

Evelyn Flynn

All my life I've been living in Cappoquin and eating Barron's bread and nowadays we are spoilt for choice. I have a B&B and always serve their bread. Lots of our guests take Barron's bread and bracks home with them.

Eileen Maher

Even though I'm from Ardmore, we always knew Barron's bread as we had an aunt married near Cappoquin and they always bought it. Deirdre was driving the van when I first came to Cappoquin and I enjoyed the chat with her and we became friends. My aunt was musical so we always appreciated Joe's lovely voice in the choir.

Catherine Begley

I'm eighty-seven years old and I remember Joe and Jack before him. They were different characters. Jack was more of a business-man in the way he acted. The van would come to our home, about three miles from Cappoquin, near The Cat's Bar. We never went to town as we could get everything from the van, even sausages and rashers. I was at the end of the line so I'd take bread for others further out. These days my grandchildren do the shopping and still buy the butter loaf, the seed loaf and barm brack. They're my favourites.

Maurice Kelleher

I'm seventy now so I'm an old boyo of the town. My main memory was of a good maths teacher called F.X. O'Leary. One of his favourite ploys to introduce decimals and fractions to students was through the idea of buying bread in Barron's. He'd say, 'If you went into Miss Barron for some Chester cake, and divided it into one hundred, and twenty was taken, what fraction would that be?' Joe Barron was a saint, not crawthumping, but he was better than any priest at leading a procession. At Benediction he would be the lead singer, along with F.X. O'Leary and Jimmy Olden, and was totally above reproach. He and Joan made an exceptional couple and they produced lovely daughters.

101

Lena Mason

Gingerbread was made on Tuesdays and I loved the smell of it. They'd cut you as much as you wanted, thick squares of it. Apple tarts were there on huge trays too, so homely. And we'd buy six pieces of Chester cake together and we'd put butter on it. I haven't seen the gingerbread for a while – if it's not still there I'll have to organise a petition to get it back! These days I buy a long pan and give my eight grandchildren bread and jam. It's always gone in no time.

Ann Carroll

Bread was delivered to us in the 1960s. We'd see the van in the distance and we'd exchange our farmer's butter for bread and brack. People were poor in those days and I don't ever remember Joe grumbling about money. Everything changed when the van went off the road. We missed the social contact, but then the shop at Melleray gates opened and Mrs Barron delivered bread there for a while. After that we went to Cappoquin for the bread and bracks.

Mary Murray

I love the country loaf and the small brown loaf with some salt and fresh scallions. The soda bread with Imogeely butter and strawberry jam is hard to beat. Esther, like her family before her, has a great presence in the community and is good at attracting interest in Cappoquin. They have been a great driving force in the Immrama Writing Festival in Lismore and the Cornerstone festival in Cappoquin. The town without the Barron's would be like *Hamlet* without the prince.

Ann McCarthy

We are neighbours with a grocery shop on Main Street and when Siobhan started to do confectionery, we were delighted. One son of mine loved the square trifles and custard slices. Both our mothers worked in their own shops and my father had Lehane's garage. We all had a lovely childhood as our parents were always there.

Maureen Hackett

I'll be ninety at Christmas and as I was born in Cappoquin, have been a customer of the bakery all my life. I entered a few competitions over the years and when I told the interviewer where I came from they would always say, 'That's where there's lovely bread.' I have a fascination for brown eggs and Hessie would always say, 'Here she's coming for the brown eggs.' She was lovely. We never had to get up early on Christmas morning as Joe Barron would cook our turkey for us. He would be up at 5am while we had the luxury of lying in. I live in Dungarvan now so I'm glad to be able to buy Barron's bread there.

Eileen Power

My father died when I was ten so I worked on the farm and I remember cycling to the town to get Barron's bread. The van would also come on a Wednesday and we had a standing order of three pans which would be left in a bag hanging on the gate. Nowadays I go to mass every day and on Fridays I go into the coffee shop for a nice cup of tea and a turnover or slice of apple tart. Often on Thursdays I buy a full apple tart and put it and some yeast buns in the freezer until I need them. We have lots of crows in nests in the trees here and even they like the leftovers of Barron's bread!

Rita Kiely

As a child I took music lessons, and not having a piano to practise on at home, I used to practise in Barron's. Practice times had to be in the evenings as Mr Barron would be in bed up to early evening. The interest he took in my music, how often I practised, whether I was getting the hang of a piece or not and awaiting the results of my exams, is a memory that has stayed with me until now. I have heard children practising, and believe me it can be torturous. He only ever gave encouragement and praise. I knew Mrs Barron much better. I grew up almost having two mothers. She was an intelligent, wise and caring woman with a wealth of knowledge on food, cooking methods and cures.

She was quietly spoken but a forceful character. She had a wonderful way about her and was respected by all who knew her.

Paddy Power

I have enjoyed Barron's bread all my life and have a clear memory of one of their wartime breadmaking secrets. Joe Barron had a few fields of about 20 acres in which, during the war years he was obliged by law to plant a percentage of in wheat. This was meant to be sent to the National Flour Mills to make into flour for the whole country. However, as Joe was my grand-uncle, my father Nicholas Power and he had a special thing going. Joe would save three or four bags of wheat from his field – he told the authorities that he had had a poor crop – and give the rest as he should to the mills. Then he would dry out his own stash of wheat over the ovens in the bakery to get rid of as much moisture as possible. When it was ready he would come on a Thursday night to my house in Williamstown, and with no-one in sight, the two of them would get a crusher going with an old oil engine. The result was a wholemeal flour which Joe mixed with his own allowance from the mills.
It meant that Joe had better bread than anyone else at the time – still not a lot, but at least he could give his customers as much as possible in very tough times. People wondered how Joe managed to

have good bread when everyone else had nothing but black bread. Well, that was how he did it.

Mary Nugent

The bread is so nice you could easily eat too much of it!

103

Dungarvan Farmers' Market, Thursday mornings

Give us this day our daily bread.

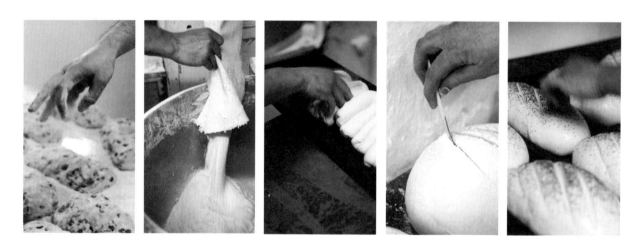

And forgive us our debts, as we forgive our debtors.

THE HOLY BIBLE

Recipes

109

Rock Cakes.

Inges.:— 2 Eggs.   6 ozs. Butter

1 lb. Flour.   1 oz. Candid Peel (chop

¼ lb. Sugar.   2 Teaspoonful. P. Powder.

¼ lb Currants & Sultanas.

Rub butter into flour, beat Eggs & add a desertspoonful of milk
mix well, stir in all other ingredients & mix with milk
and egg, which will become just damp. Butter a large
tin and place the mixture on it in small rough looking
heaps. and bake in a quick oven.

Queen Cakes.

Inges.:— 2 Eggs. 1 cup Flour. ¼ cup. Butter.
3/4. tbs. Teaspoon B. Powder.

Cream butter & Sugar drop in one egg & mix with a
little flour, drop in second egg & beat well with remain
of flour, lastly add B. Powder and mix all well if
too thick add a little water. Bake ¼ hour in a hot oven

Devonshire Apple Cake.

Make about 1 lb of Short Crust, grease a soup plate and cover with a layer of the crust. Peel core and cut up some Sour Apples, place half of them on the plate pastry sprinkle with Demerara Sugar and add a clove or two. Damp the edges of the pastry and cover with a second layer of Pastry. Add the rest of the Apples and a third layer of crust and Cook in a hot oven until crisp & golden. This too may be served either hot or cold, with Cream.

Baked Marmalade Pudding.

Make some pastry, line the sides of a pie-dish with it then cover the bottom with Marmalade. Beat two eggs with ½ pt milk and add a cupful of breadcrumbs and a little grated Lemon rind. Pour this over the Marmalade in the dish, and bake for 3/4 of an hour.

Mushroom Soup in a Blaa

Serves 4

This is an easy recipe and quantities of ingredients don't have to be exact, so you can avoid using the weighing scales. I serve this in a crusty roll, such as one of Barron's traditional blaas. The bread taken out of the roll to make space for the soup is used as breadcrumbs to thicken the soup. The cut-off tops can be buttered or dipped in olive oil.

2 handfuls mushrooms, chopped

1 large onion, finely chopped

1 clove garlic, finely chopped

Knob butter

500ml water or stock

1 handful breadcrumbs

Chopped parsley

½ teaspoon chopped chilli or chilli flakes (optional)

Splash milk or cream (optional)

In a saucepan with the lid on cook the onions, garlic and mushrooms in the butter until the onion is soft. Add the stock which can be chicken, beef or vegetable, or water with a dash of soya sauce. Gently simmer for 10 minutes.

Cut the tops off four rolls. Remove most of the inside, leaving a thick enough crust to hold the soup. Brush the inside with melted butter and place in the oven for 10 minutes at 180°C, 350°F, GAS 4 to crisp up a little.

In the meantime, make breadcrumbs from the insides of the rolls.

To finish the soup add the breadcrumbs and cook for a further 5 minutes until the soup thickens and becomes deliciously creamy.

Add a splash of milk or cream to finish if you fancy it, and top with chopped parsley and/or chilli in winter.

Spoon the soup gently into the rolls and serve.

113

Spinach and Bacon Salad with Croutons

Serves 4

Dandelion leaves can replace spinach in this recipe, which is also good for using up leftover bacon or ham bits.

125g young spinach leaves, stalks removed

4-5 streaky rashers, uncooked

2 cloves garlic, crushed

3 tablespoons wine vinegar

2 hard boiled eggs, quartered

Freshly ground black pepper

2 slices bread, cut into squares

Fry the squares of bread with one of the cloves of garlic in a little oil until golden. Remove from the pan and set aside.

Wash and dry the spinach and place in a salad bowl.

Fry the chopped rashers in the pan, adding a little oil if necessary and toss around until browned, or heat leftovers in a frying pan.

Add the other clove of garlic and cook for a minute. Pour the hot bacon over the spinach.

Add the vinegar to the pan and heat, scraping any bits collected at the bottom. Pour over the greens, add the hard boiled eggs and lots of pepper. Finish by adding the garlicky croutons.

115

Welsh Rarebit

Serves 4

Originally called Welsh Rabbit, for no reason connected to the bunnies, it became a rare bit in the 18th century to reflect its tastiness. There are plenty of versions of this dish from England, Wales, Scotland and France from the simplest cheese on buttered toast to this one.

250g cheese

1 teaspoon butter

2 teaspoons Worcester or soya sauce

1 teaspoon dry mustard

2 teaspoons flour

4 tablespoons milk or beer

4 slices bread

Salt & pepper

Toast the bread on both sides. Grate the cheese into a saucepan and heat gently until it melts. Add the other ingredients and mix well. Spread over the toast and grill until brown. Garnish with chopped parsley and serve at once.

Bread with Tomato

Serves 4

This simple toasted bread with tomato can be made as complicated as you like. In Spain they call it Pan con Tomate and sometimes top it with dried ham and/or anchovies. It is always drizzled with good quality olive oil to finish which makes it silky and delicious.

4 slices thickly cut bread

2 tomatoes, halved

1 large clove garlic

Olive oil

Optional:

4 slices dried ham (serrano, pata negra)

8 canned anchovies

Salt and black pepper

Toast the bread until golden.
Rub with the garlic clove, using the rough toast like a grater. Rub with the halved tomatoes right down to the skin so the pulp rubs off the toast.

Drizzle the toast with olive oil and sprinkle with salt, ideally crunchy flakes, and pepper.

If liked, top with a slice of dried ham and/or a few anchovy fillets. Serve while the toast is still crisp.

Picnic Loaf

Serves 10-12

Barron's basket loaf is ideal for this, but any good quality unsliced loaf will do.

The filling is a matter of preference. I have given my easiest tasty one here, but don't hesitate to improve on it. You may like to add some chopped chillis, red peppers or paprika to add spiciness. I like the addition of rocket for peppery flavour, or some chopped coriander or parsley. Don't skimp on the quantity. I like toasted almonds with salmon or trout too. The beauty of it is it can be prepared a day in advance of any party and is quite a treat for special picnics. There is no problem with omitting the prawns or shrimps, or using crabmeat with less salmon as both are rich. Chopped capers or gherkins are delicious too.

1 crusty bread loaf, unsliced

1 fillet fresh salmon, cooked

Juice half a lemon

Handful olives, pitted and chopped

3 large tomatoes, chopped and drained of juice

Handful cooked peas

Handful cooked prawns or shrimps

Handful lettuce leaves, shredded

Few rocket leaves

3-4 tablespoons mayonnaise, ideally homemade

Cut the end of the loaf and cut around the inside to loosen the bread inside. You just need the crusty shell for this treat, so make the inside bread into breadcrumbs and freeze to use later. Cut into the bread, leaving half an inch (about 1cm) all around the inside, making sure you don't perforate the crust as the filling will leak out. Err on having it too thick inside.

Flake the salmon in a bowl and mix with all the other ingredients.

Pack the mixture inside the loaf shell, pressing down so it becomes compact. Overfill it a little, then press in the sliced-off lid, trimming it so it fits inside. If I find the filling doesn't come up to the top, I replace some of the bread on top which nicely soaks up the excess juices.

121

Cover with foil or clingfilm and sit a weight such as a can of food on top so it compresses a little. Leave upright in the fridge overnight or until needed. To serve, cut into slices or spoon out, cutting a little of the crust for everyone as you get down through the loaf. Accompany with a green salad, dressed with olive oil and lemon juice.

Tomato Salad
with Squidgy Bread

Serves 3-4 as a starter

This salad comes from Italy, but you will see versions in Spain, Greece and all along the Mediterranean. It's one of those clever dishes which uses up leftovers beautifully while making the best of tomatoes when in season. The idea is for the bread, stale or fresh, to soak up the delicious salad juices while giving the salad substance. It's a great way to use up stale bread which is even better than fresh.

100g cherry tomatoes, halved

1 slice bread, cut into cubes

1 small red onion, sliced finely

100g feta cheese, crumbled

Handful olives

1 teaspoon balsamic vinegar or wine vinegar

1 tablespoon olive oil

Handful fresh oregano leaves, chopped mint, basil or tarragon

Salt and freshly ground black pepper

Mix all the ingredients together and if possible, allow the flavours to blend for about 10 minutes before serving.

Stuffed Tomatoes

Serves 2-4

This is my own recipe born of necessity to feed many on very little to hand in the kitchen. It's amazing how far a few rashers can go when there is bread in the house.

4 large tomatoes

2 slices bread

2 spring onions, finely chopped

2 streaky rashers, chopped

Skim of oil

Thyme

Salt and freshly ground black pepper

1 egg (optional)

Preheat the oven to 180°C, 350°F, GAS 4.

Heat a frying pan, add a little oil and the rashers. Fry until crisp.

Make the bread into breadcrumbs. In a bowl mix with the rasher pieces, spring onions, some fresh thyme, or a few fresh leaves of any kind – basil and oregano work well. Season with salt and pepper.

Adding an egg makes the mixture bind better, but the recipe works without too.

Take the tops off the tomatoes and set aside. Scoop out the seeds and carefully cut into the membrane so you have a smooth space to take the filling. Add the membrane into the bread mixture, and even the seeds if you like. At this point you can also add any leftover bits of cheese, fish or cold meat.

Spoon the mixture into the tomatoes and replace the tops.

Place in the oven. Don't be fussy about temperatures and if you are cooking something else, use the heat for it. Just watch it if the temperature is higher than I have suggested. They take about 15 minutes for the tomatoes to sizzle deliciously.

Serve with a green salad, pepped up with a little seasonal rocket and, to make a meal of them, with creamy, mashed potatoes.

125

Summer Pudding

Serves 6-8

This is a superb way of using up stale bread in a stylish, colourful way, making the best of seasonal fruit. My recipe uses any blend of fruit as long as it's juicy and ideally has some red or black colours such as raspberries, strawberries, blueberries and blackcurrants.

6-8 slices thick, stale white bread, crusts removed

750g mixed berries

75g sugar

Place the fruit and sugar in a saucepan and heat slowly at first until the sugar dissolves. Bring to the boil and simmer for 3 or 4 minutes or until the fruits burst and release their delicious juices.

Allow to cool and add more sugar to taste if necessary.

While the fruit is cooking, line a 1.5 litre pudding bowl with most of the bread slices, reserving some for the top. Overlap the slices rather than leave a gap. Tip in the fruit and drizzle the juices down the sides of the bowl so that it is drenched. If there is any leftover it's a good idea to reserve it to cover bare patches when you un-mould later.

Cover with the remaining slices of bread and fit a plate snugly inside the bowl. Set a weight such as a few cans of beans or bags of sugar to compress the fruit.

Keep in the fridge or a cool place for a day or two until required. To serve, tip gently onto a serving plate and drizzle with leftover juice. Decorate with fresh fruit or drizzle with fresh cream.

Baked Fruit on Bread

Serves 4

Use up stale or leftover fresh bread with this delicious simple recipe from France. While usually used with peaches, apricots and plums, it's also delicious with gooseberries, blackcurrants and raspberries.

2 slices bread, buttered

2 peaches or nectarines

4 apricots or plums

2 heaped teaspoons butter

2 heaped teaspoons brown sugar

Heat the oven to 180°C, 350°F, GAS 4.

Butter the bread on one side and cut each slice into three or four.

Grease an ovenproof dish well and place the bread in it, butter side up.

Halve and stone the fruit, cut into quarters and place on the bread pieces.

Put the butter and sugar onto the fruit and bake for 25 minutes until the bread will be golden and the fruit coated with a delicious syrup.

Mrs Barron's Orange Pudding

Serves 4-6

This pudding looks as good as it tastes, with its soft orange flavour and light, spongy texture. It can be made well in advance and heated before serving. If you are good with microwaves, it's worth experimenting with cooking it for 15 minutes on medium to high with a plate right side up to cover it. Allow it to rest and turn out to test. It can easily be popped back into the bowl to cook further.

90g butter

90g caster sugar

2 eggs

120g plain flour

½ teaspoon baking powder

Juice 1 orange

Grated rind 2 oranges

Beat the butter and sugar until light and creamy. Add an egg and half the flour and beat well. Add the other egg and the remainder of the flour and the baking powder, along with the orange rind and juice. Stir lightly.

Pour into a 2 pint or 1 litre pudding bowl, cover with greaseproof paper or tinfoil, tie with string and place in a saucepan half filled with water. Steam gently for 2 hours.

Serve hot.

Mrs Barron's Fig Pudding

Serves 6-8

This is a rich, naturally sweet pudding which should follow a light meal. Use a small teacup or half a mug to measure. This can be microwaved, but with different power it's difficult to say for how long. Try 25 minutes on medium to high.

100g butter

100g sugar

1 egg

1 cup milk

1 teaspoon lemon juice

2 cups flour

1 teaspoon baking powder

¼ teaspoon salt

1 ½ cups dried figs, chopped

Cream the butter and sugar in a bowl.

Mix the egg and milk and add. Sieve the flour, salt and baking powder into the mixture, then add the figs and lemon juice.

Pour into a 2 pint or 1 litre pudding bowl, cover with greaseproof paper or tinfoil, tie with string and place in a saucepan half filled with water. Steam gently for 2 hours.

Serve with custard flavoured with lemon juice or white wine.

Mrs Barron's Marmalade Tart

Serves 6-8

At home, Joan Barron referred to this recipe in the more general sense as her marmalade pudding, but it's really more a tart with a pudding topping, and delicious it is too. The tart orange flavour contrasts beautifully with the softer custard-like topping which is a good foil for the crisp pastry. Any bought or homemade pastry will do – shortcrust is ideal and I have given my own recipe which is quite crumbly. It is too difficult to roll out, so simply press pieces of it into the tart tin. It cuts well too. Make it before preparing the filling.

Pastry

1 egg yolk

110g butter

375g plain flour

1 dessertspoon caster sugar.

Filling

2 eggs, beaten

2 tablespoons marmalade

150ml milk

90g white breadcrumbs

Grated rind ½ lemon

Mix all the pastry ingredients together to a crumbly texture and squeeze in the hand to bring it into a few balls. Press each ball into a 26cm tart tin or flan dish. The pastry can be easily patched if it breaks up. Refrigerate for an hour to firm up.

Preheat the oven to 180°C, 350°F, GAS 4.

Cover the base of the pastry case with the marmalade.

For the filling beat the eggs and milk. Add the breadcrumbs and lemon rind. Just before putting into the oven pour the filling onto the marmalade base. Bake for 45 minutes when the topping should still be soft, but a little firm.

135

Serve on its own with cream or custard.

Mrs Barron's Apple Betty

Serves 4-6

Another excellent recipe for using up breadcrumbs, this one cannot fail and is ideal to try with children who are learning to cook.

250g soft breadcrumbs

500g cooking apples, peeled and chopped

150g light brown sugar

1 teaspoon ground cloves and cinnamon, mixed

50g butter

Preheat oven to 180°C, 350°F, GAS 4.

Butter a baking dish.

Arrange alternative layers of apples and breadcrumbs, sprinkling each layer with brown sugar, cloves and cinnamon. The top layer should be breadcrumbs.

Dot well with butter and a sprinkling of sugar.

Cover with foil and bake for 45 minutes. Remove the foil and allow to brown for 10 minutes.

Serve warm with whipped cream.

Mrs Barron's Devonshire Apple Tart

Serves 6-8

This recipe comes from Mrs Barron's well-worn recipe book and is a perfect comfort food.

French Pastry:

300g plain flour

150g butter

150g caster sugar

2 egg yolks

Filling:

4-6 cooking apples

100g demerara sugar

4 whole cloves

Mix all the ingredients for the pastry except the flour together to a loose dough, then add the flour. Add a little milk if too dry. Squeeze with the hands until in a ball. It may seem dry at first but the heat of the hands will make it stickier. Don't work it too much or it will become leathery when cooked. Divide into three pieces and wrap in foil or clingfilm and keep cool until ready to use.

Preheat oven to 180°C, 350°F, GAS 4.

Roll out each third of pastry into discs to fit a soup plate, baking dish or sponge tin. Patch it up if it breaks, don't be fussy about it. Peel, core and cut the apples into chunks.

Grease the plate or tin and place one third of the pastry on the bottom.

Add half of the apples and two of the cloves and sprinkle with half of the sugar.

Sit another third of the pastry on top and cover with the rest of the apples, sugar and cloves.

Top with the last third of the pastry and pinch the edges of the pastry together to seal. Decorate with any bits of leftover pastry. For an extra golden finish brush with milk, a mixture of a beaten egg and some milk, or leave and it will still become light golden.

Place in the hot oven and bake until crisp and golden – about 40 minutes.

Dust with caster sugar while still hot.

Serve hot or cold, with or without cream.

139

Mrs Barron's Bread and Butter Pudding

Hard to beat on a cold winter's night, bread and butter pudding can be made with a variety of fruits, crystallised ginger, soaked prunes, even chocolate. The term used years ago for bread that wasn't fresh was 'settled'. For this recipe it can have 'settled' even for a week. Use Mrs Barron's basic recipe first – it's hard to beat.

1 800g white sliced pan, ideally a few days old

1 orange rind

175g sultanas

110g sugar

50g margarine or butter

850ml milk

3 eggs

Grease a large dish. Bring the sugar, margarine and milk to the boil in a saucepan and leave to cool.

Remove crusts from bread. Butter each slice. Lay one layer of bread in dish, butter side down. Grate some rind of orange over and sprinkle a third of the sultanas on top.

Put another layer of bread on top of this, orange rind and another third of the sultanas.

Repeat so you now have 3 layers of bread.

Whisk eggs into the cooled milk mixture. Pour over bread and cover with cling film. Leave to soak for approximately 1 hour.

Remove cling film and bake in oven at 200°C, 400F, Gas 6 for 50 to 60 mins.

Serve hot with custard.

141

Carrot cake

Esther got this recipe in 1980 from her friend Mary Curran te Kloot, who lives in the outback in Australia. Esther reports that her friend fell madly in love with an Australian sheep farmer, packed her bags and, adventurous and courageous as always, left the safety of home for a new life on the other side of the world. It was Mary's idea to get the confectioners at Barron's to experiment with her recipe. Now it's one of the bakery's best sellers.

115g grated carrot

125g sultanas

170g granulated sugar

125g wholemeal flour

1 teaspoon bread soda (bicarbonate of soda)

1 teaspoon cinnamon

2 large eggs

100ml vegetable/sunflower oil

Simple Icing

100g sieved icing sugar

1-2 teaspoons boiling water

Preheat oven to 190°C, 375°F, GAS 5.

Mix together the carrot, sultanas, sugar and flour in a bowl. Sieve the cinnamon and bread soda into the mixture.

Beat the eggs and vegetable oil together for 3 to 5 mins. Add to the other ingredients. Beat together for 5 to 10 mins.

Butter and line a 1lb (500g) loaf tin with greaseproof paper and spoon in the mixture.

Bake in the preheated oven for 40-60 mins. Cool on a wire tray, then remove paper.

Mix the icing sugar and boiling water together to form a soft paste and cover the top of the cake.

Decorate with cherries.

143

Sponge Sand...

Inges:- 6 ...

Orange Marmalade.

Inges:- 2 doz. Seville oranges. 3 sweet oranges.
2 Lemons.

Wash fruit & wipe, cut oranges cross ways and remove
all the pips, cut them into a bowl and cover with boiling
water. Squeeze out juice and put into another bowl — put pith
& oranges into preserving pan, put the peel through a
cutter & also add to preserving pan — then add water until
... is nicely thin to stir — steep over night or longer, and
then boil for about 1 to 1½ hours. Put pips on to boil with
... water that is poured over them, then strain off water &
add it to preserving pan, also juice — then measure and for
each pint of fruit add 1 lb. sugar, and boil for 1 hour a...
... set when tested on a cold plate.

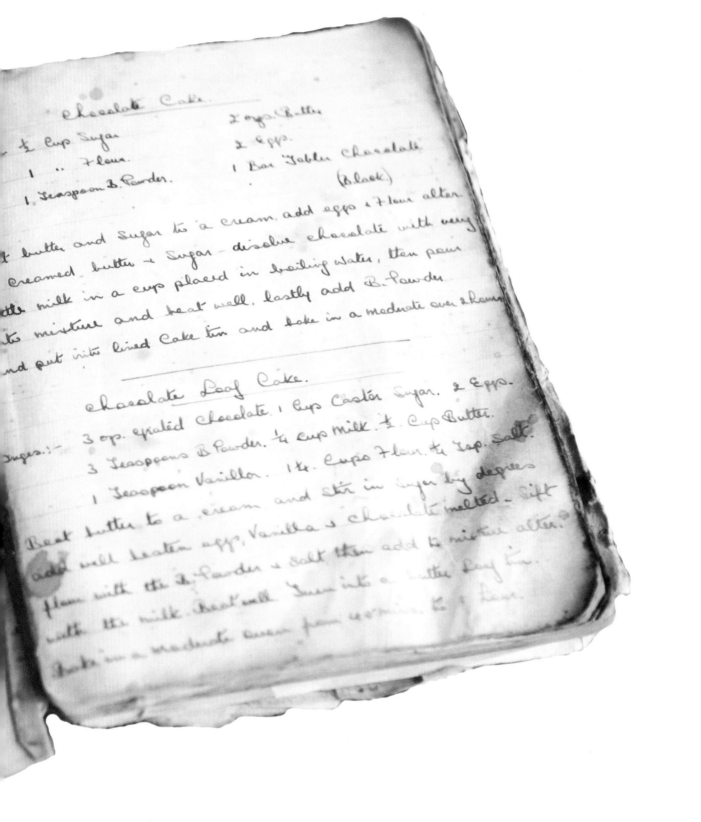

Chocolate Cake.

½ cup Sugar.   2 ozs Butter.
1 " Flour.   2 Eggs.
1 Teaspoon B. Powder.   1 Bar Table Chocolate
          (Black)

... butter and Sugar to a cream, add eggs & flour alter...
creamed butter & Sugar — dissolve chocolate with very...
... milk in a cup placed in boiling water, then pour...
... mixture and beat well, lastly add B. Powder...
... put into lined Cake tin and bake in a moderate oven 2 hours...

Chocolate Loaf Cake.

Ingres:— 3 ozs. grated Chocolate. 1 Cup Caster Sugar. 2 Eggs.
3 Teaspoons B Powder. ¼ cup milk. ½ Cup Butter.
1 Teaspoon Vanilla. 1½ Cups Flour. ¼ Tsp. Salt.
Beat butter to a cream and stir in Sugar by degrees
add well beaten eggs, Vanilla & chocolate melted — Sift
flour with the B. Powder & Salt then add to mixture alter...
with the milk. Beat well. Turn into a butter loaf tin.
bake in a moderate oven from ...... to 1 hour.

Index

147

With bread and wine you can walk your road

SPANISH PROVERB

Arna Run Runarsdottir
is a Winchester-based professional
photographer. Her work includes
corporate photography in Denmark and
Iceland and food photography in France.
This is her first time working in Ireland.
An award winner in Edinburgh, she has
taught photography in Iceland and
exhibited there and in Gallery 94
in London. She is engaged to an Irishman.

Roz Crowley is a freelance writer
and editor. She is based near Blarney
in Co. Cork.

"Once you start,
there is no end
to who is to go in
and who
is to be left out."

GEOFFREY FISHER